# MORE
# SHOCKING
## AND SURPRISING
### *Somerset Stories*

# MORE
# SHOCKING
# AND SURPRISING
## *Somerset Stories*

JACK W. SWEET

*Somerset Books*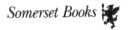

First published in Great Britain in 2002

**British Library Cataloguing-in-Publication Data**
A CIP record for this title is available from the British Library

ISBN 1 86183 466 6

SOMERSET BOOKS
Official publisher to Somerset County Council

Halsgrove House
Lower Moor Way
Tiverton, Devon EX16 6SS
Tel: 01884 243242
Fax: 01884 243325
email: sales@halsgrove.com
website: www.halsgrove.com

Printed and bound by
MPG Books Ltd, Bodmin

# CONTENTS

# DEDICATION

To everyone who made this book possible, and to all Somerset folk.

*Meet me by moonlight alone,*
*and I will tell you a tale.*
*Must be told by the moonlight alone,*
*In the grove by the end of the vale.*
Joseph Augustine Wade (1796?–1845)

# ABOUT THE AUTHOR

Jack Sweet was born in Yeovil and has lived most of his life in the town and county of many of his ancestors. An old boy of the former Yeovil School, he joined the staff of the Yeovil Borough Council on leaving the Royal Air Force in 1958. After working as a professional local government administrator, he took early retirement following thirty-four years' service with the Borough Council and its successor, the South Somerset District Council.

Jack Sweet has always had a great love of history, and for many years has been writing articles for local publications, including the weekly *Yeovil Times* and South Somerset District Council's monthly *News and Views*. His first book *Shocking Somerset Murders of the Nineteenth Century*, published by Somerset Books in 1997, is now in its second edition, and in 1999 Somerset Books published the first *Shocking and Surprising Somerset Stories*.

In addition to his writing, Jack Sweet is interested in local and family history, photography, voluntary work in the Museum of South Somerset, and has visited many former battlefields from South Africa to the Crimea, via the United States of America and Northwest Europe. He is married to Margaret and they have three daughters and a grandson.

# ACKNOWLEDGEMENTS

My many thanks to Robin Ansell of Yeovil Reference Library, and David Bromwich and staff of the Somerset Studies Library, for their invaluable help during the preparation of this book.

To Michael Shorter, ARPS, for preparing many of the photographs.

To Peter Waters, Editor of *Somerset Life*, and Martin Heal, Editor of the *Western Gazette*, for permission to reproduce the articles acknowledged in the Sources.

To Marion Barnes, of the Museum of South Somerset, for permission to use photographs nos 2, 7 and 23.

To the Bath & North East Somerset Library and Archive Service (Bath Central Library) for permission to use photograph no. 6.

# PHOTOGRAPHS

All the photographs used in the book belong to the author unless shown below.

2, 7, 23, Museum of South Somerset; 6, Bath & North East Somerset Library and Archive Service (Bath Central Library).

# INTRODUCTION

My second book of *Shocking and Surprising Somerset Stories* spans the three centuries from 1645, and the chaos of the English Civil War, to the shock of the German air raids during the Second World War of 1939 to 1945. I tell of the true events and personal stories which could have shocked, surprised and in some cases, perhaps raised a smile on the faces of the folk who lived in this Land of Summer.

I am very proud of my Somerset birth, and many of my forebears would have known and been affected by some of the events of which I tell. An ancestor was out with Monmouth in his Rebellion of 1685, my late father fought on the Western Front in the First World War and was an air raid warden during the raids on Yeovil in the Second. The adventures of my great-grand-father, James Martin, are recounted in the floods of 1894.

So please read on, and I hope you will enjoy my *Shocking and Surprising Somerset Stories*.

# THE DEADLY BELLOWS MAKER

There is a fine view to the west from the churchyard of St Andrew's, Ansford, near Castle Cary, and in the distance, the Tor of Glastonbury rises above the Somerset Plain in a scene little changed since the diarist Parson James Woodforde preached here over 200 years ago. The church, however, might not be immediately recognisable to the parson, as it was entirely rebuilt in the 1860s and only the tower remains from its medieval past.

James Woodforde was born in 1740 in the Parsonage at Ansford Hill and would have walked to the church down a lane which now bears a name once familiar in the village – and once notorious. Tuckers Lane, apart from a short narrow length which rises from Lower Ansford, is now a modern estate road but still forms the main access to St Andrew's from Ansford Hill. The names of roads and streets usually concern themselves with everyday subjects such as local features, churches, famous people or heroes, battles and so forth, but Tuckers Lane remembers something more sinister – a murder.

Reginald Tucker surveyed the sea of faces below him, and having been told the crowd on Kewards Green at Wells, on this September afternoon in 1775, was over 10,000, he was determined to give them a show they would remember and tell their grandchildren. He handed the prayer book back to the white-faced clergyman standing by the steps and, with a careless gesture, pulled off his cravat and tossed it away. Tucker then opened the collar of his shirt, took the noose from the hands of the waiting hangman, slipped it over his head and around his neck. For a moment he stood looking at the crowd, contemplating perhaps, the chain of events which had brought him to this spot, and then there was nothing beneath his feet.

Reginald Tucker was born fifty years before, in 1725, and brought up in the village of Huish Episcopi near Langport. His father died when he was a child and when old enough, he was apprenticed to a bellows maker in Wells. The young Tucker was clever and learnt the trade quickly, but being a wild youth, and deciding that bellows' making held no excitement, ran away to become a soldier. He saw active service in Scotland during the 45 Rebellion of Bonnie Prince Charlie, and was wounded at the Battle of Culloden.

With an honourable discharge from the Army, and a small pension for his wound, Tucker returned to Somerset where he joined his mother in keeping the Ansford Inn. However, he was by no means the genial host, and soon acquired a reputation for fighting and quarrelling with customers and neighbours. In 1750, no doubt to the relief of many, Reginald Tucker married, and with his new wife Martha, departed for London where he set up business as a bellows maker. Being a clever craftsman, he was soon making a good living from the sales of a ventilator of his own design, and for the next eighteen years he lived the life of a prosperous businessman in a house off The Strand.

Then a strange thing happened. There was a disastrous fire which completely destroyed Reginald Tucker's house and business premises but, as everything was fully insured, he received a substantial payout for his loss. Several rich Jews were lodging in the house at the time and they lost a very large sum of money in the fire; or so it seemed. Rumours were soon in the air, however, that Tucker had stolen the cash but no action was taken against him for lack of evidence.

Suddenly Reginald Tucker was a much richer man, and left London in 1771, returning to Ansford with his wife, son and daughter, to live in a house in the lane which led to St Andrew's church. Back in the village some twenty years later, his reputation for violence had not lessened, and soon there was gossip that another son had been born to the family when they were in London but the child had been killed in his mother's arms by a blow aimed at his wife during an argument.

The Tuckers had been living in Ansford and worshipping at St Andrew's some four years, farming and receiving the income from the rents of fields, when on 8 June 1775, things went terribly wrong. No one will ever be sure what exactly happened on that day, but without doubt there was a vicious quarrel between the couple which resulted in Martha being beaten to death, and to Reginald Tucker appearing before the Somerset Assizes at Wells on 25 August charged with her murder.

The indictment alleged that Tucker had struck his wife on the back of her head with a sledgehammer, with fatal results. In his defence he swore his innocence, explaining to the court that the couple had lived in complete harmony for more than two years, and therefore he had no cause or reason to beat his wife. Tucker also tried to throw the blame onto several local people with whom he had quarrelled.

The prosecution witnesses, of which there were many, testified as to his strange appearance and unusual demeanour on the day of the murder, and it was alleged that Tucker had been seen at the Nine Wells washing blood from his shirt. When questioned as to how bloodstains came on his coat, he explained that about a week before the fatal day he had collected his daughter from a friend's house, and on returning home the front door had slammed with such force that two panes of glass had fallen out. Tucker went on to say that on the following day he had sent to Castle Cary for a glazier to repair the door but in the meantime he had begun to hook out the putty. In the process he had cut one of his fingers and had wiped the blood off on his coat.

A report of the trial states that Tucker appeared to be in complete control of himself, only showing emotion as his bloodstained coat and the sledgehammer were produced in court, when he was seen to shed a few tears.

Despite continued protestations of innocence, the jury found Reginald Tucker guilty, and at five o'clock on 25 August, the Judge sentenced him to be executed and his body given for dissection to a surgeon in Langport.

Parson Woodforde, recorded in his diary that the trial had lasted ten hours, and he had been summoned as a witness to testify to Tucker's character but when his name was called he was out at dinner and so failed to appear. However, he believed the prisoner to be guilty, and presumably his absence did not affect the outcome of the trial. As Tucker was taken away still protesting his innocence, Parson Woodforde commented that if he was innocent he would be amply rewarded in heaven, but if not – then the Lord be merciful to his soul.

On Monday 4 September, in the late afternoon, the condemned man received the Holy Sacrament three times, but, although he continued to declare his innocence of the murder of his wife, he was reported to have said that during his life he had been guilty of other offences which had deserved death.

Reginald Tucker climbed into the cart which would carry him to the place of execution with the deepest alertness and seeming unconcerned. He was dressed in deep mourning and accompanied by a clergyman, he carried a prayer book in his hand, which he read all the way from the prison to the gallows.

At about five o'clock on that September afternoon in 1775, Reginald Tucker was launched into eternity in front of 10,000 spectators on Kewards Green.

They took the body down from the gallows, placed it in the waiting hearse which began the slow journey to the dissecting table at Langport – Reginald Tucker was going home.

# AN AUTUMN STORM

Captain George Cope, of the ketch *Emma* did not like the look of the weather as he beat down the Bristol Channel bound for Highbridge with a cargo of coal late on Tuesday afternoon 1 October 1895. The *Emma* had sailed from Lydney earlier that day in company with the Gloucester ketch *Hereford*, whose master was Captain Thomas Guy, also carrying coal to Highbridge. In Walton Bay off Clevedon, with the wind beginning to blow hard from the south, Captain Cope hailed the *Hereford* and announced to Captain Guy that he would make for Cardiff roads to ride out the weather rather than continue to Highbridge. The two ships parted company at about six o'clock, and the *Hereford* continued on her way to catch the early morning tide into Highbridge wharf.

Although the wind was strong from the south all that Tuesday evening, there was little to indicate that it would be more than an autumn 'blow', and perhaps Captain Cope's fears would be groundless; also no storm signals had been raised along the north Somerset coast. However, by about ten o'clock, the southerly wind became squally, at midnight it calmed, and then it roared out of the northwest with a violence described as the heaviest storm experienced on the Somerset coast for many a year. The storm reached its raging height between two and three on the Wednesday morning when, according to the *Bridgwater Mercury*, it blew with the force of a hurricane.

In Bridgwater Bay, a number of ships were waiting to catch the flood-tide to take them into the mouth of the River Parrett, and up the river to Highbridge or Bridgwater. Running before the storm, the ketch *Eliza* of Cardiff, making for Highbridge with a cargo of coal, and the coal ketch *Providence*, destination Bridgwater, were in the channel of the River Parrett off Burnham, with their sails blown away. The strong flood-tide raised and powered by the storm, swept the two vessels out of control up the river until they smashed into one another. So severe was the collision, both ketches began to sink under their crews who managed to escape into the *Providence*'s undamaged ship's boat and reach the shore below Highbridge Pill without loss.

At about half past eight on Tuesday evening, Captain Crossman, master of the screw steamer *Tender* bound for Bridgwater with 150 tons of Welsh coal, brought his vessel to rest on the mud north of Stert Island to await the flood-tide which would take the small ship up the river. Just after two o'clock, with the storm increasing in fury, the *Tender*, with full steam up floated off the mud, but suddenly the stern swung and was caught in the mud. The steamer heeled over onto her starboard side and into the raging surf. With giant waves breaking over the stricken vessel and sweeping her deck, Henry Hawkes, the mate, and fireman, Frederick Dennison, managed to launch and clamber into the waterlogged ship'ss boat. Despite their frantic efforts to reach the master and engineer, the small boat was carried away in the savage current and deposited its terrified cargo on the beach above Highbridge Pill.

Back on the *Tender*, Captain Crossman and the engineer, George Harding, were clinging to the bridge with the huge seas pushing the ship further and further onto her starboard side. With no hope of rescue in the black of the storm-tossed night, and with the stricken steamer filling rapidly with water, Captain Crossman put on a lifebuoy, shouted to the engineer to grab a plank or ladder to save himself, and jumped overboard. For nearly an hour he was swept up the River Parrett, but despite passing several ships at anchor, he could not attract attention in the howling dark. However, more dead than alive, Captain Crossman was finally rescued by the crew of the *Princess May*. Of George Harding, the engineer, there was no sign.

The steamer *Bulldog*, en-route to Cardiff from Bridgwater, had anchored off Burnham, but at the height of the storm her anchor chain broke and she was driven onto the Berrow Flats. Fortunately, the vessel was not overwhelmed by the huge surf, and her crew scrambled ashore at daybreak. The *Bulldog* was refloated several days later and taken to Cardiff to be overhauled. The pleasure yacht *White Wings*, moored by Burnham Pier foundered in the storm without loss of life, and a number of fishing boats were damaged and their gear washed away.

The sloop *Tom* of Watchet, was carrying stone from East Quantoxhead to Minehead, and at the time the storm broke was anchored off Minehead waiting for the tide. As the wind increased in fury, the anchor began to drag and the sloop was being blown back across Blue Anchor Bay. Off Dunster beach, the crew slipped the anchor, set a small sail, and ran for the shore as it would have been impossible to beach the vessel near Watchet. As the *Tom* touched ground, the crew launched the ship's boat and with great difficulty landed on the beach. Despite their efforts, the crew could not haul the sloop above the high-water mark, and abandoning their efforts for the night walked home to Watchet. At daylight, the men returned expecting to find the *Tom* smashed to pieces in the surf, but the sloop had disappeared without trace!

George Clapp, the Burnham pilot, had a narrow escape in the storm. In company with William Howe, he had set out in the pilot boat *Halloa* to a vessel called the *Jinks* waiting in the bay. The pilot later recalled that, 'There was scarcely any wind when we left the pier, and we had got about half-way out from where we had seen the previous evening the vessel which we were going to pilot up the river, when, all of a sudden the wind flied round to the northwest with all the fury of a tremendous gale. In fact, it came at us like a clap of thunder, and we were almost blinded with rain at the same time, besides being pitchy dark. Our boat at once became perfectly unmanageable, and we could do nothing but drive back with the boat at the mercy of the sea, which nearly swamped us. We were driven up the river at great speed against the Huntspill sea wall, and as soon as the boat struck we managed to jump ashore. In less than two minutes afterwards my boat as again dashed against the wall with tremendous violence and knocked into a thousand pieces.' The two men walked back to Burnham, and despite their near fatal ordeal, joined the crew of the Burnham lifeboat, the *John Godfrey Morris*, which had just been summoned.

During the storm, the Burnham lifeboat had been on standby, but in the pitch black of the storm no one could establish whether any vessels were in trouble. However, in the first light of Wednesday morning, the fate of several ships could be seen. The steamer *Tender* was capsized off Burnham, two vessels were sunk in the river just below Highbridge Pill, a ketch and another sailing ship could be seen in possible trouble some five miles distant beyond Stert Flats, and the steamer *Bulldog* was ashore on Berrow Sands.

Mr G.B. Sully, the Lloyd's agent, and Mr Stoate, the secretary of the Lifeboat Institution at Burnham, considered that more than one lifeboat was needed, but when at six o'clock they sought to telegraph the lifeboat stations at Watchet and Weston-super-Mare, to their surprise the postmaster advised that under Post Office Regulations contact by wire could not be made before eight o'clock under any circumstance. However, all was not lost, and following the postmaster's suggestion, the officials of the Great Western Railway at Highbridge provided telegraphic communication with the two towns, and the *C.H. Kingston* was launched from Watchet, and the *John Holt* from Weston-super-Mare.

The *John Godfrey Morris* was launched from Burnham at about a quarter past six, with George Clapp and William Howe in the twelve-man crew. Although the full fury of the storm had abated, the wind was still blowing hard and the seas heavy as the lifeboat, under sail, tacked up the river to the wrecks of the two coal ketches. Establishing that the crew were safe, the lifeboat returned down river and made for the vessels seen in trouble out in the bay. However, it was not until about nine o'clock that the Burnham lifeboat finally came alongside the first, which was identified as the ketch

*Hereford*. Wallowing in the heavy breakers but still anchored, the ketched appeared to be abandoned, and after taking the *John Godfrey Morris* in as close as he dared, Coxswain Alfred Hunt satisfied himself that there was no one on board, and the three-man crew and the ship's boat were missing. The *Hereford*'s sails had been torn away and the deck swept clear, but because of the breaking waves it was deemed too dangerous to put men aboard and take the ketch into harbour.

The Burnham lifeboat then set out for the second vessel seen in distress, and the mystery of the *Tom* was solved. The sloop, still with the small sail set, had apparently refloated during the night, and been blown into Stolford Bay. With a number of the lifeboatmen as temporary crew, the *Tom* was sailed back to Burnham.

The Weston-super-Mare lifeboat had stood off the *Bulldog* until it was confirmed that her crew were safe, and the Watchet lifeboat stood by their Burnham colleagues at the *Hereford* and *Tom*.

Later on Wednesday, the *Hereford* ran onto the Stert Flats and broke up in the surf. Her boat was found smashed against the Huntspill sea wall, but of Captain Thomas Guy and Amos Rawles and William Daunton, his crew, there was no sign. The engineer of the steamship *Tender* was also missing.

On Friday 4 October, the body of William Daunton was found on Stert Island by George Clapp, the Burnham pilot, who also identified the corpse of the man he had known for over twenty-five years. At the inquest which followed in Highbridge, there was speculation on the fate of the crew of the *Hereford*. They could have been swept off the ketch by the heavy seas and drowned, or lost in the ship's boat. No one could ever know, and a verdict of 'found drowned' was returned on the corpse of William Daunton.

A week after the storm, the body of Captain Thomas Guy was found in the River Parrett near Combwich, and the corpse of Amos Rawles recovered off Stert. At both inquests, the speculation of the fate of the two men continued, but once again the result was inconclusive, swept off the *Hereford* or lost in the ship's boat. Verdicts of 'found drowned' were returned.

The badly decomposed corpse of the fourth man to be lost in the storm off Burnham, the engineer of the *Tender*, George Harding, was recovered many miles up the River Parrett at Burrow Bridge on 17 October. Identification was by the clothing and stature of the engineer, and the verdict of the inquest was 'Accidentally drowned through the upsetting of the *Tender* steamship for which no one was to blame'.

The *Tender* was salvaged and, after a refit, gave many years service to her owners, Messrs Sully & Co. of Bridgwater, until she was broken up in 1942.

# A FATAL FOOTBALL GAME

It looked as if the football match on Saturday 29 March 1902, between the Yeovil Harlequins Football Club 2nd XI and Stoford, would be called off because some of the Harlequins had not turned up. The two teams, however, agreed to play a practice match at the Stoford pitch, and kicked off. The Stoford players were in a boisterous and pugilistic mood and after a few minutes the Yeovil men threatened to leave the field. However, everyone soon calmed down and the game continued, but not for long.

The ball was centred and a Stoford player, twenty-year-old baker William Murley, sprinted to gain possession but collided violently with Harlequin Arthur Meaden. The Stoford player rebounded heavily into burly sixteen-year-old Harlequin Francis Pragnell, just as he was about to kick the loose ball, and being thrown off balance, his elbow struck William Murley in the left side and his knee came up into William's stomach. The force of the blow knocked William Murley to the ground but he got up and walked off the pitch. After a while he began to complain of stomach pains and was helped to his home in Stoford. William Murley took to his bed feeling unwell and during the next few days his condition deteriorated. On the afternoon of Tuesday 1 April, despite the attention of Dr Colmer and his assistant Dr Clarke-Baylis, William Murley died.

The inquest into William Murley's death was held by the Coroner, Mr E.Q. Louch, on 3 April at the old refreshment rooms in Stoford. The first witnesses were the two Harlequin players, Francis Pragnell and Arthur Meaden, who described the game and their collision with the deceased. Both denied deliberately striking and kneeing William Murley and emphasised that there was no foul play, no foul had been called by the deceased, the Stoford team or the referee. Arthur Meaden stated that several of the Stoford team were rather excited, and he had not been keen to play because he believed at least one of them was the worse for drink and there was a good deal of cursing and swearing. However, William Murley had played a fair game and the witness had nothing to complain about his play.

Following the evidence of Pragnell and Meaden, the Coroner adjourned the inquest until the following Saturday because he had an appointment in Frome and had not anticipated the inquiry would take so long.

The first witness at the adjourned inquest was Randolph Churchill, a local gamekeeper, who stated that he was playing for Stoford in the supposed match. He suggested that Francis Pragnell had deliberately charged into William Murley but then admitted that he had not called foul. Churchill also revealed that the referee was an eleven-year-old boy! In reply to the Coroner, the witness admitted that he had been a little excited when he came on the pitch and had had a glass or two of liquor with William Murley before the game. However, Randolph Churchill denied shouting 'Break their...legs,' and had not used any bad language. The witness had helped William Murley home, and confirmed that on no occasion had his injured team-mate accused anyone of deliberately hitting him. The Coroner once again asked Churchill if he was drunk and the witness replied, 'I was not drunk and I was not sober.'

The next witness was sixteen-year-old Stoford lad Herbert Badland, who stated that he was linesman for the match and had been standing only 2 yards from the collision. He had seen Pragnell run up to Murley and charge him with his right elbow which had knocked the deceased around, and Pragnell had then brought up his left knee into William Murley's right side. Badland considered that this was a foul charge but admitted that he had not called foul because the referee was not a proper one and he did not hear anyone else call foul.

Dr Clarke-Bayliss, assistant to Dr Colmer, testified that he had been called to the deceased on Sunday afternoon and found him complaining of severe pains in his left side and abdomen. The patient had described the collision at the previous day's match and said that it had been an accident.

The last witness was Dr P.A. Colmer who stated that his post-mortem examination had found a perforation of the deceased's small intestine about the size of a shilling piece, and the cause of death was acute peritonitis. He considered that the injury had been caused by the circumstances described in the evidence.

Following Dr Colmer's testimony, the Coroner addressed the jury and stated that he was aware that they were all Stoford men and a Stoford man had died, but he was certain they would come to the right conclusion. *Pulman's Weekly News* reported that the Coroner went on to say that:

In outside games, such as cricket and football, the laws allowed a little keenness on the respective sides, but on this occasion there seemed a little more than keenness. At the start there was some hesitation as to whether the game should be begun at all, and the Harlequins considered from the attitude of some of the Stoford players they were a little excited, especially one named Churchill. From the way in which the latter had given his evidence and the admission he had made he (the Coroner) thought he would not be inaccurate in stating he was drunk, and they must utterly disregard any statement he had made as to what occurred on that occasion, as his mind was not that of a man who could receive an intelligent account. The singular thing was that although the Stoford players had told them distinctly they considered Pragnell was playing outside the ordinary laws of football, none of the players said a word about it. There was no referee worth calling, but a boy who ran about with a whistle, and the boy did not blow his whistle. Not a single player raised a voice in reprobation of what Pragnell was alleged to have done. Churchill and Murley did not speak of Pragnell when the deceased was assisted home, and it must be clear that the accident as it then occurred was regarded by Murley as one of the ordinary accidents of football. It stood to reason that if Pragnell had done intentionally what it was alleged he did, there would have been a unanimous exclamation of a foul, and that would have been the one topic to talk about. They could dismiss from their minds any deliberate attempt on the part of Pragnell to commit serious injury or to use such violence in the course of the game towards that player as to practically knock him out. If it could be proved there was such an intention on his part then undoubtedly he did commit manslaughter. Pragnell had given his evidence in a straightforward manner. Murley did receive a blow, and Meaden said the deceased cannoned from one to the other, and they did not show that it was anything beyond the ordinary rules of the game. It was regrettable that the injuries Murley received had terminated fatally, but it was satisfactory to know that Murley had said it was a pure accident of football, and he did not allege foul play. If there had been any suggestion of foul play it would have lingered in his mind. From the evidence he thought they would arrive at the conclusion that the injuries were brought about by an accident, and that there was no intention on the part of Pragnell to commit wanton and deliberate injury.

The Stoford Jury returned a verdict of 'accidental death' and no blame as attached to anyone. William Murley was buried in Barwick churchyard on Saturday afternoon, 5 April 1902, and four Harlequins were amongst the mourners.

# DEATH DOWN THE PIT

The night shift at Bray's Down Colliery, near Dunkerton, was making ready to descend into the pit on 22 June 1843, to earn another meagre day's pay in the Somerset Coalfield. They were Job Richardson, aged thirty, married with no family, Richard Aylesbury, twenty-three and single, Jacob Richardson, thirty-six, with a wife and six children, Aaron Dando, aged twenty-eight, married but no family, Thomas Aylesbury, twenty-five, married but three months, Richard Pickford, twenty-one, Jeremiah Filer, aged sixteen, and eleven-year-old John Ashman.

The miners climbed onto the chain at the end of the winding rope and sitting or standing in the loops they had attached by iron hooks to the chain, waited for the loading planks to be drawn back from the mouth of the shaft and begin their decent to the pit some 400 feet below. The signal was given to lower away, the steam engine hissed, machinery began to rumble as the winding drum was put into gear, the planks pulled back, and the eight miners began their descent into the dark; just another routine shift under the green hills of Somerset.

Suddenly, the drum wheel began to revolve faster and faster until it was spinning out of control, and the winding rope with its human cargo plunged screaming down the shaft to crash onto some staging projecting a few feet above the bottom of the pit. Six miners died, but miraculously Richard Pickford and young John Ashman survived the fall, seriously injured.

The inquest before the County Coroner, Mr Uphill, was held at the Red Post Inn, about ½ a mile from the the Bray's Down Colliery, and the first witness was the chief engineer William Lewis. He told the jury that he had been fitting some new parts to the steam engine, and on the afternoon of the accident he had carefully examined the machinery and found it to be in perfect order. Mr William Wait, the managing proprietor of the colliery was with him at the time, and the engine was working when he went home at about half past five. The engineer stated he had been told of the accident at half past eight that evening and had rushed back to the colliery. On arrival, West, the engineer working the machine, had told him that for some unaccountable reason the drum had become disconnected from the main wheel. William Lewis stated that he asked West if he had put in the plug to keep the drum of the engine in gear because this was missing. West had confirmed that he had put the plug in place but when asked where it was, he could not say. The witness believed that West understood his work, and had not been drinking.

Job West, the engineer, was the next witness and said that he had been working the engine to pump water from the pit, and had finished at about six o'clock. He had put the engine into gear in readiness to let the men down at eight o'clock, and when he did so, he had put in the plug. A plate had to be placed over the plug and screwed down to prevent the plug from becoming detached. Whilst the witness could remember securing the back nut of the plate, he could not recall securing the front. Before he let the men down, he had moved the engine two or three times to pump out any water in the machine in order to make it safe. West stated that after the men had been let down about 100 feet, he saw the drum running, but it was too late to do anything to stop it. He had worked the engine for nearly a year at night, and his brother worked it by day.

The bailiff of Bray's Down Colliery, John Berryman, recalled giving the men their candles, and as they were drawn up he had removed the planks from the mouth of the shaft. The engineer had announced the engine ready, and at his instruction the shift was lowered. The bailiff stated that suddenly he heard cries of alarm from the shaft, and saw three-hundredweight of rope spinning off the drum and disappearing down the pit. He believed the men had fallen about 300 feet. A new rope was attached, and he sent four men down to see what could be done. They found five men dead, one would die shortly after, and two were brought up dangerously injured. John Berryman stated that the engine must have been in gear or it could not have let the men so far down, and nothing of this kind had ever happened before.

This was the whole of the evidence, and after a short deliberation, the jury returned a verdict of 'accidental death'.

The *Bath Chronicle* described the appearance of the bodies as:

> not such as might have been expected from the horrible manner in which death had been occasioned; with the exception of Richard Aylesbury, the faces of the deceased presented no evidence of the fright-ful catastrophe which had suddenly hurried them into eternity; their appearance being more that of persons who had died peaceably in their beds, some of their countenance being actually impressed with a smile. The deceased were men of honest, sober, pious, and industrious habits.

The newspaper further reported that the machinery had sustained damage costing about £50 to repair, and many of the cogs had been broken off the wheels.

About a week after the accident, eleven-year-old John Ashman died from his injuries, but Richard Pickford, who had suffered a broken leg, was said to have been on his way to recovery.

# POACHERS AND POLICE

In the summer of 1893 gangs of poachers were at work in the Sherborne and Yeovil areas and the local police were on alert. One suspected poacher, Frederick Moors of South Barrow, had been seen in Sherborne on Friday evening 14 July, and his horse trap was parked in the yard of James Lyne's house in Bristol Road. Lyne was a convicted poacher, and the local constabulary suspected that something was in the air.

At about five o'clock the next morning, Sherborne constable P.C. Payne, was patrolling the Bristol Road when in the early dawn light he saw a trap coming towards him at a fast pace. As it drew nearer the constable recognised Frederick Moors as the driver and James Lyne in the passenger seat but as he shouted 'Halt!', Moors whipped the horse into a gallop and disappeared down the Bristol Road. However, as the trap passed, P.C. Payne glimpsed a large sack bag in the back of the vehicle.

Five miles away at Yeovil Bridge, four police officers were also on poacher alert: P.C. Meech of Yetminster and P.C. Miller from Nether Compton were concealed behind hedges at the bottom of Babylon Hill and P.C.s Marsh and Wise from Yeovil were on the Somerset side of the bridge.

At about 5.30am the officers saw a trap being driven quickly down Babylon Hill and as it approached the bridge, the driver and his passenger were recognised as Moors and the convicted poacher Lyne; a large bag could also be seen in the back of the trap. P.C. Miller ran out into the road with raised hands, shouting for the driver to stop, but Moors swerved the trap around him and urged the horse into a gallop. At this moment P.C. Meech rushed from his hiding place tried to seize the reins from the driver but missed and fell under the trap. The constable was knocked unconscious and dragged for several yards but as his body was freed from the trap, one of the wheels of the speeding vehicle ran over him.

The trap raced over Yeovil Bridge and P.C.s Marsh and Wise were forced to jump for their lives as it drove furiously towards them and disappeared up the Sherborne Road to Yeovil. Despite their narrow escape, the two constables had time to glimpse a large bag in the back of the trap.

All this was witnessed by Thomas Score, the dairyman at Yeovil Bridge Farm, who was standing on the bridge at the time, and who would later corroborate in court the statements of the policemen; he would also confirm that there was a large bag in the back of the trap.

P.C. Meech recovered consciousness but was badly hurt and bleeding heavily from a head wound. He was taken to Dr Williams in Sherborne and after treatment for severe lacerations to his back where the wheel had gone over him, a deep scalp wound and heavy bruising, the constable was taken home.

Later that Saturday, Frederick Moors and James Lyne were arrested and taken into custody. On 20 July the two men were brought before the Sherborne Magistrates charged with causing grievous bodily harm to P.C. Meech and assaulting the officer in the execution of his duty. The events of the Saturday morning were recalled by the prosecution who stated that the police officers had tried to arrest the prisoners on suspicion of poaching. The four constables described their actions and those of the prisoners, and Thomas Score recounted what he had witnessed as he stood on Yeovil Bridge. Yeovil solicitor, Mr W. Marsh, defending, stated that before the police had the right to stop his clients, they must have good cause to suspect that they had come from land where they had been in search of game. The fact that James Lyne had once been convicted of poaching did not justify the attempts to stop his clients without proper authority, and the police must take the consequences of their actions. His clients had been lawfully driving to Yeovil, the constables had suddenly jumped into the road, frightening the horse, which broke its rein and ran away out of control, accidentally knocking down P.C. Meech. Mr Marsh therefore sought the dismissal of the charges. However, the Magistrates committed the prisoners for trial but allowed bail at £25 each with two sureties of £25.

Frederick Moors and James Lyne appeared at the Dorset October Quarter Sessions. Despite further pleas that there was no proof that they had been on a poaching expedition (the sack contained mushrooms), and that because the police had no authority to seek to arrest the two men, the injuries to P.C. Meech had been the result of an unlawful act on his part and therefore accidental, they were found guilty and sentenced to nine months hard labour.

P.C. Meech made a full recovery from his injuries.

# THE FORGER OF MARK

It was Bridgwater Fair Day, 24 June 1818, when a man entered Mr Foster's shop and asked to buy a knife. In payment he handed a one pound bank note, payable on the Bristol & Somersetshire Bank, to Ann the shopkeeper's daughter, who lacking sufficient cash in the till, took it to the next-door neighbour, Mr Trood, to change. However, Mr Trood refused to oblige, and so Ann went to the bank where Mr Thomas Paul looked at the note and also refused to change it. In fact, Mr Paul appeared very unhappy with the note and, after sending for the town constable, accompanied Ann back to her father's shop where the customer was patiently waiting for his change. On being asked where he had obtained the bank note, the customer replied that he had taken it from an unknown man in payment for some shoes. Not satisfied with the answer, and knowing the note to be a forgery, Mr Paul requested the constable, who had just arrived at the shop, to take the man in custody to the Town Magistrates.

The customer's identity was quickly established as George Nuttycombe, a resident of the village of Mark, and a search of his person produced 140, one pound notes payable on the Bristol & Somersetshire Bank, all forgeries. The magistrate, the Reverend Dr Wollen, despatched Mr William Counsell, clerk to solicitors Messrs Poole and Stradling, armed with a search warrant and accompanied by a town constable, to search the Nuttycombe family home at Mark, some 9 miles from Bridgwater.

The arrival of the two men at the house in Mark disturbed Robert Fry, a Bristol pipe maker, in the process of printing more bank notes, and he was taken in custody back to Bridgwater. In the meantime, Henry Puddy, George Nuttycombe's brother-in-law, had been arrested for passing forged Bristol and Somersetshire Bank notes in Bridgwater.

On 13 August 1818, George Nuttycombe and Robert Fry appeared before Mr Justice Park at the Somerset Assizes in Wells, charged with forging and uttering a promissory note purporting to be a note of the Bristol & Somersetshire Bank. If found guilty they would hang, but their accomplice, Henry Puddy, had turned King's Evidence to save his neck, and would be the Crown's principal witness.

Mr Abraham Moore opened for the prosecution and after outlining the case called his first witness, Thomas Nuttycombe, to the stand. Thomas Nuttycombe stated that George Nuttycombe was his son who had come to live at his home in Mark last May. On 17 June, Robert Fry had arrived and had stayed at his house until 24 June when he was arrested. At his son's request, Fry had been given one of the two bedrooms in the house to sleep in by himself, and the witness, his son and daughter Maria had shared the second. A man called Davies, who seemed acquainted with his son and Fry, had called on 21 June, stayed overnight with Fry, and left the next day. Thomas Nuttycombe recalled seeing a wooden board in Fry's room and on being asked what it was, Fry had told him it was for grinding colours for painting earthenware or china. He had never seen Fry working on the board.

Maria Nuttycombe followed her father and said that she had also seen the board but had never seen Fry working on it.

The next witness, James Luff from Mark, a carpenter, stated that both prisoners had called at his master's shop on 20 June and, following Fry's instructions, he had made a wooden framed board about 5½ feet long by 8 inches wide. Fry had paid 5s.6d. for the article, and on leaving he had told the witness that if anyone asked what he had been making he should reply that he worked for money and not for knowledge. James Luff identified the board forming the printing press produced in evidence before the court as the one he had made for Fry.

John Spencer, the next witness, stated that he was a turner living in Wedmore, and recalled that on 20 June, George Nuttycombe had called at his workshop and asked him to make a pair of rollers. This he had done, and several hours later both prisoners came back to his shop. Fry had examined the rollers and said that they would do very well, and after paying two shillings the two men had left. John Spencer pointed to the rollers on the press and stated that these were the ones he had made for George Nuttycombe.

Willian Counsell, the clerk to Messrs Poole and Stradling, took the oath and described how, on 24 June in company with Joseph Keen, the constable, he had been sent with a warrant from the Magistrate, the Reverend Dr Wollen, to search Thomas Nuttycombe's house in Mark. He stated that the house consisted of three rooms on the ground floor, one on each side of the front door and a lumber room leading off the left- hand room. Access to the two bedrooms on the first floor was gained from stairs in the left-hand room; there was no back door.

Mr Counsell stated that when he entered the house, Maria Nuttycombe was alone washing clothes in the right-hand room, and Joseph Keen told her that her brother had been arrested in Bridgwater for forgery and they had come to search the house. Nothing incriminating was found in the two downstairs rooms, but the search of the back room disclosed an apron heavily stained with a black substance which resembled printer's ink. Almost immediately the constable found a man hiding behind a projecting part of the wall and dragging him out, demanded his name and business. After some hesitation the man disclosed that he was Robert Fry, a potter, and asked why his hands were black, replied that he had been blacking shoes even though none could be seen in the house.

Mr Counsell stated that two local men were summoned and Fry placed in their custody whilst a search was carried out of the bedrooms. In the inner back bedroom, which they had been told Fry occupied, they found a bench resting on two boxes, and an iron pot on which some charcoal was burning under a gridiron. Nearby was a palette knife, a jar of printing ink and a printing ball. On the window ledge there was a parcel of paper cut to the size of a bank note and across the room several string lines had been stretched from a beam to hooks over the window. In the corner they found the printing press, which was now before the court, and underneath the bed was a large quantity of notes purporting to be of the Bristol & Somersetshire Bank, and which appeared to have been recently rolled off. A search of the second bedroom disclosed the copper plate used for printing the notes, hidden under a mat. Mr Counsell stated that he had searched Fry and found a genuine Bristol & Somersetshire Bank one pound note. A second search of Fry's room produced a box containing 21 Bristol and Somersetshire Bank one pound notes, dated, filled up and signed, two partly filled up notes and 75 blanks. In conclusion, William Counsell stated that an impression made from the plate compared exactly with the notes found in Fry's bedroom.

The next witness, Ann Foster, described the events of 24 June in her father's shop when George Nuttycombe had sought to change the one pound note.

Thomas Paul, the banker, stated that he was well acquainted with the handwriting of all the partners and clerks of the Bristol & Somersetshire Bank, and immediately he had seen the note presented by Ann Foster, he knew it to be a forgery.

William Bindon, the entering clerk of the Bristol & Somersetshire Bank, told the court that he had been shown the notes found on Nuttycombe and they were obvious forgeries.

The next witness was Henry Puddy, the brother-in-law who had turned King's Evidence to save his neck. He testified that on 23 June, George Nuttycombe had told him that a man called Fry was printing bank notes at his father's house, and asked him to go with him to Bridgwater Fair the next day to pass them. Agreeing to the plan, Puddy recalled going to the Nuttycombe's house where he saw Fry printing the notes in the bedroom. He watched as Fry put some ink on the copper plate, then lay one of the cut pieces of paper on it and pass the plate between the rollers after which he took off the note and hung it up to dry. When the note was dry, Fry filled in the blanks and George Nuttycombe trimmed the edges with a knife. Puddy stated that the notes were of the Bristol & Somersetshire Bank.

The next day he had gone with George Nuttycombe to Bridgwater Fair and on the way he had been given some of the notes. In Bridgwater he had bought a handkerchief at a shop in Eastover, another had been passed for a 'pick item' on the town bridge, and opposite the town gaol he had bought a quarter-pound of blue dye with a third note; he had then given all the change to George Nuttycombe. With a fourth note he bought a pair of stockings, and shortly after he had been arrested.

With Puddy's evidence, the Crown closed its case, and apart from pleading not guilty and George Nuttycombe producing two character witnesses, neither accused made any statement in their defence.

The jury found George Nuttycombe and Robert Fry guilty of forgery and they were sentenced to death. On 2 September 1818, before a large crowd outside Ilchester Gaol, Nuttycombe and Fry were hanged by the neck until they were dead.

For Robert Fry, it seems that his execution for forgery had only been deferred, because five months before in April 1818, he had pleaded guilty to forgery at the Bristol Assizes, but due to 'a chasm in the chain of evidence, the jury acquitted him'. Some people never learn!

# A FOE FOR A FRIEND

The church of the Holy Cross, Weston Bampfylde, stands on a low hill south of Sparkford, and would seem at first glance to be an unlikely candidate for the echoes within its walls of surprising events, political intrigue, government agents, double dealing and Robinson Crusoe.

On the south wall of the nave there is a memorial to Grace, the daughter of Matthew and Ann Lydford of Weston Bampfylde, wife of Nathaniel Mist, and who died in 1726, aged thirty-six years at Carter Lane, London. On the memorial her grieving husband penned the following epitaph to his beloved Somerset wife:

> *In prisons and dungeons her resolution and fidelity were his comfort and support whilst her mildness and other conjugal vertues sweetnd his better fortunes.*

What did Nathaniel Mist mean when he penned these words for the monument he erected to 'preserve the memory of her who made his life happy'?

Little is known of the early life of Nathaniel Mist except that he was probably a Wiltshire man by birth, and served as an ordinary seaman in the Royal Navy in the Spanish Seas. He first comes to notice when he set up as a printer in Carter Lane in the City of London in 1715, the year following the succession of the Hanoverian George I to the throne of England, and in 1716, Mist founded the *Weekly Journal* supporting the Jacobite cause of the deposed Stuarts. The Jacobites had made a serious attempt in 1715 to place James III, the son of the ill-starred James II, who was known as the Old Pretender, on the English throne, but the uprising was swiftly suppressed. However, there was continual plotting against George I, and the Jacobites' readiness to advance their cause whenever they could, including the use of anti-government propaganda and journals, was a constant source of anxiety to the Government. The Jacobite cause was finally destroyed in 1746, when the Old Pretender's son, popularly known as Bonnie Prince Charlie, and his army were defeated at the Battle of Culloden.

It was into this atmosphere of plot and counterplot, that Nathaniel Mist, the ex-seaman, introduced his Jacobite newsheet, which was soon selling some 10,000 copies every week to a large proportion of the reading public of the time. Another figure now appeared on the scene and became editor of

Mist's *Weekly Journal,* the enigmatic Daniel Defoe. As plain Daniel Foe, he was the son of a London butcher and claimed to have ridden with the Duke of Monmouth in the Rebellion of 1685. He trained to be a Dissenting Minister, was a businessman, a bankrupt, a pamphleteer and journalist, the author of *Robinson Crusoe* and *Moll Flanders*, and the pioneer of the English novel, before dying in hiding from his creditors in 1731. The mysterious Defoe was also a government secret agent serving both Tory and Whig governments at various times! For at least ten years before becoming editor of Mist's *Journal* in 1716, Defoe had been working as an undercover government agent and had spent some time in Scotland operating against the Jacobites in 1706 and 1707.

Defoe's mission in joining Nathaniel Mist was to gradually neutralise the *Journal* by softening its Jacobitism, and render it harmless without raising the publisher's suspicions. He wrote the anti-government editorials and on one occasion a raid and search of Nathaniel Mist's home produced the originals of the seditious articles in Defoe's handwriting. Later, Defoe would boast that he had so softened the *Journal's* tone that it was becoming useful to the Government. Needless to say, even with Defoe writing the articles, Mist could not escape attention, and he was arrested and thrown into gaol or put in the pillory on several occasions for libels against the Government. Each time, however, Defoe would intercede for his employer and either obtain his release or the reduction in the severity of the sentence. How could Nathaniel Mist suspect that his loyal editor could be anything but a friend and supporter of the cause?

Although by 1724 Mist had been in and out of gaol several times, he continued to be a thorn in the side of the Government, but it was during his last imprisonment that somehow he finally discovered Defoe's duplicity. On his release, an extremely angry Nathaniel Mist went looking for his editor with murder in mind and on finding Defoe, drew his sword and laid into him. In the fight which followed Mist was wounded, and Defoe called a surgeon to dress his opponent's wounds, but whether this was done through pangs of conscience for his one time colleague, or from the basic fear that if Mist died, he would be in serious trouble, both history and Daniel Defoe are silent. In 1728, some two years after the death of his wife, Mist's position had become very dangerous, and now lacking Defoe's protection, he fled to France where he died nine years later from asthma.

# LOVELY WOMEN, FAIR BUT FALSE

George Brooke, described by the *Western Flying Post* as 'A bill sticker, an old man well known in the town', appeared before the Yeovil Town Magistrates on Friday 14 September 1866, charged with stealing the sum of 6s.3d. from Jane Kean.

Jane Kean told the Bench that on Wednesday 12 September, in company with George Brooke, she had gone into the Half Moon public house in Silver Street, and called for two half-quarters of gin. She had taken a golden sovereign (£1) from her purse to pay for the drink which came to 6d., and the defendant had received the change of 19s.6d. pence which he had put in the purse and given it back. Jane Kean stated that she had then gone into the parlour and sat down with the old bill sticker. Later, when she had looked into her purse, she found that 6s.3d. was missing but had to admit that she was very tipsy at the time. In reply to George Brooke's solicitor, Mr S. Watts, Jane Kean also admitted that she could not remember whether or not she had invited the defendant to accompany her into the Half Moon, but she was certain that she had not given him her purse – he had taken it and put it in his pocket.

The next witness was the barmaid of the Half Moon, a Miss Cross, who stated that George Brooke and Jane Kean had come in together, and the woman had called for gin for which she had paid 6d. The couple had then gone into the parlour and shortly after Jane Kean called for two more half-quarters of gin for which she emptied her purse, containing one sovereign, onto the table. Miss Cross took the coin and returned with the gin and 19s.6d. change in silver coins. She saw George Brooke put the coins into the purse and hand it to his lady companion. Later, however, Miss Cross, who could see into the parlour from the bar, observed the bill sticker take the purse and put it into his pocket. He had then shaken the pocket, pulled out the purse and hand it back to Jane Kean. The barmaid told the Bench that she had become suspicious that something was not quite right, and when George Brooke made to leave she had told him to sit down, and she sent for the police. Miss Cross went on to say that Jane Kean had been drinking and did not seem to know what was going on.

Police Constable Everley told the Bench that he had been called to the Half Moon, and found the defendant and Jane Kean, who was drunk, sitting in the parlour. George Brooke was sober and when questioned denied having any change belonging to the woman. Despite this denial, the constable searched the defendant and found 6s.3d. in silver coins in his pocket.

Mr Watts then addressed the Magistrates on the defendant's behalf. He admitted that his client had the woman's money, but he had been holding it at her request. He could only account for the change being found in his pocket because the purse had no fastening and some of the coins had fallen out by accident. Mr Watts stated that his client had a good character for honesty, and if the charge was proved against him he would lose his club benefit.

The Mayor, who was Chairman of the Town Magistrates, asked the defendant if he had been in Sherborne on the day in question and how much he had drunk? In reply, George Brooke confirmed that he had, and stated that he had drunk two half-pints of half-and-half. When he had arrived back in Yeovil he had seen Jane Kean who had called out to him, 'Come here my dear, and show me the way to the Half Moon.' George Brooke told how he had taken the woman to the public house and had accepted her invitation to have some gin, provided she paid. They had both gone in and Jane Kean, who was very tipsy had sat on his lap and twice fallen off. The defendant explained that when he had handed back the purse after paying for the gin she had said, 'Thee shall have it and I too'. Every time he tried to leave, Jane Kean had pulled him back and would not let him go.

After a short consultation with his fellow Magistrates, the Mayor addressed George Brooke saying that this was one of those drunken cases which perplexed the Bench as to how they should deal with it. With the exception of being too fond of drink, the defendant had a good character, and it was because of this the Bench was inclined to be lenient. Believing that the money might have been accidentally emptied into his pocket, and what he had done was through drink and not with any felonious intention, the case was dismissed but at the same time George Brooke was cautioned to keep out of bad company, to give up drinking, and avoid lovely women, fair but false.

# THREE SHOCKING MURDERS

Thomas Laver of Ilton was a very careful man and saved for his old age from his meagre labourer's wages. In fact he was so careful, it was said that 'by hard labour and a most penurious mode of living (frequently eating with hogs), he had accumulated nearly £40 in cash which he always carried about with him sewn up in his pockets.' Thomas Laver's fortune was so well known in the area that no one was very surprised when on the evening of the 15 December 1798 he was found battered to death, his pockets cut open and his money gone.

Suspicion fell on two local villains, Richard Williams and James Podger, who had been overheard saying that they would not mind killing Thomas Laver for his money, and who had now disappeared from their usual haunts. Warrants were issued for their arrest and a month later a letter was intercepted from James Podger to his relatives in Ilton asking for his box of clothes and some money to be sent to a public house at Mile End Green in London.

The Ilminster postmaster and a local gentleman accompanied the box to London where they sought the assistance of the Bow Street Magistrates to effect the arrests. Two Bow Street Runners, the postmaster and his companion, Podger's box and a third Runner disguised as a porter, made their way the public house. The porter entered and was met by Richard Williams who confirmed that his friend James Podger was expecting the box and, on being identified by the postmaster, was arrested. Shortly after Podger arrived back at the public house and was taken into custody. Despite both men vehemently denying any knowledge or involvement with the murder, the Bow Street Magistrates were satisfied with the evidence of identification given by the Ilminster postmaster and his companion, and the accused were committed to prison pending their return to Somerset.

Only Richard Williams stood trial at the Somerset Assizes charged with the murder of Thomas Laver – James Podger had turned King's Evidence and escaped the fate of his erstwhile companion, who was found guilty and sentenced to death.

Richard Williams was hanged in April 1799 at Ilton acknowledging the justice of his sentence, while Podger disappeared into the mist of time.

Farmer Styling was tired as he returned home to his farm in the small village of Goathurst, near Bridgwater, late in the evening of Wednesday 15 November 1809. After a long day helping a neighbour sow his wheat, he was looking forward to supper in the warm farmhouse kitchen. However, as Farmer Styling entered the yard, he was puzzled to find the barn doors wide open, and going into the house, was horrified to find his twenty-seven-year old wife, Sarah, lying on the kitchen floor in a mess of smashed crockery and blood – dead. The shocked farmer also found that his young farm servant, Thomas Gage, had disappeared and his mare was missing from the stable. A search of the farmhouse discovered the theft of two £10 notes, some silver coins and spoons, a greatcoat, some dresses and a gun with powder and shot. A closer examination of Sarah's body revealed that she had been killed by a vicious blow from an axe or hatchet to the back of her head as she sat at the kitchen table.

A hue and cry was raised for the murderer and robber, and within a short time the farmer's mare, much driven and minus saddle and bridle, was found grazing quietly on Brendon Hill. Two days later, the missing farm servant was discovered hiding near his parent's home in the Exmoor village of Brompton Regis, and it was established that Thomas Gage was in fact Thomas Tarr, who had absconded from his apprenticeship in the village during the previous June. However, none of the stolen cash or articles were found with him.

Thomas Tarr was brought back to Goathurst and examined by the local Magistrates. Pleading his innocence of the crime, Tarr stated that some little while before, he had been riding a horse owned by Mrs Styling's father and had driven the animal so hard that it had fallen and subsequently died. His mistress had threatened to send him to gaol, and on the afternoon of the murder he saw two men come into the farm yard. Fearing they had come to take him to gaol, Tarr explained that he had fled from the barn where he had been working, and made his way on foot to his home. He suggested that the men might have been the murderers and robbers. In the fall from the horse Tarr had hurt his leg, but the examining Magistrates were not convinced that he could have walked the many miles to Brompton Regis with such an injury. Neither were they convinced that he was telling the truth, and he was committed to Ilchester Gaol to await his trial at the next Somerset Assizes.

On Monday, 2 April 1810, eighteen-year-old Thomas Gage, alias Tarr, appeared at the Somerset Spring Assizes in Taunton, and was found guilty of the murder of his mistress, Sarah Styling, and then robbing her house, and sentenced to death. Seven days later the young murderer was hanged at the Stone Gallows, near Taunton, having confessed his guilt a few hours before the fatal drop.

᠙᠙᠙

Mr Metford of Glastonbury, a woollen stocking manufacturer, employed outworkers in Wells and the area around the city, and every Saturday, Robert Parsons delivered the wool, and collected and paid for the finished stockings. On Saturday, 10 December 1815, Robert Parsons, with help of James Marsh, another of Mr Metford's employees, loaded up the covered delivery cart with the bags of wool and placed the £12 cash for the wages by his driver's seat. Just before he was about to leave, James Marsh, who had been sent to feed his employer's cattle, came running up and asked the carter if he could ride with him to Wells. No objection was raised and they set off for the city.

Half-way between Glastonbury and Wells, some labourers were at work in a brickyard, when they heard the faint shouts and sounds of a struggle coming from a covered cart they could see some way off on the high road. As the cart travelled on towards Wells, the sounds of the struggle became more violent and were followed by the loud shrieks and groans of someone in great distress. The workmen dropped their tools and went to render assistance, but as they approached the cart they saw a man dragging an apparently lifeless body from the vehicle and into the roadside ditch. Shouting 'murder' the men ran towards the cart, and the supposed assassin jumped over the hedge and made off across the fields as fast as he could run. The workmen found Robert Parsons lying dead in the ditch, badly beaten and with his throat shockingly cut from ear to ear. Whilst several of the men remained with the body, one of them went in pursuit of the fleeing figure, and just recognised the fugitive before he lost sight of him behind some hayricks; it was James Marsh whom he had known since they were children.

James Marsh was quickly taken into custody and on Friday 5 April 1816, he appeared at the Somerset Spring Assizes in Taunton, charged with the murder of Robert Parsons. Marsh was found guilty and sentenced to hang at Ilchester Gaol on Monday 8 April, following which his body would be sent for dissection.

The *Taunton Courier* reported on 11 April that:

On the road from Taunton to Ilchester, Marsh behaved in a most hardened and audacious manner, and throughout that day was equally violent and abusive to all who came near him. On Sunday he appeared very unconcerned at chapel, but during that day he was less abusive. On Monday he was visited early by the Rev. Mr Reece, chaplain to the gaol, to whom he acknowledged the crime for which he was to suffer, but declined assigning any motive for it. He appeared less insensible to his situation than before, but refused the sacrament. At nine, his brother-in-law was admitted to visit him, of whom he took leave in a very careless, unconcerned manner. At a quarter before eleven he was removed from the chapel, and on turning round to shake hands with his brother convicts appeared affected. From thence he proceeded to the platform, and as usual the chaplain first ascended the drop, the prisoner immediately followed, and had no sooner arrived there, then finding the chaplain about to call him to prayers, he said, 'no, I shall say no more – where is the man,' (meaning the executioner,), 'I am ready.' He however was prevailed on to kneel down and join in prayer, but in less than three minutes he rose up in the middle of a prayer, and again called for the man. The chaplain descended, and the executioner got up to perform his sad office, during the performance of which the prisoner frequently said, 'make haste'. He was however left about two minutes, when he again said, 'I am ready', and instantly fell. He died without a struggle. During the time the executioner was placing the rope around his neck the prisoner thought it was not properly placed and told the executioner to put it a little further back. Thus perished this desperate murderer in the twenty-third year of his age, almost as melancholy an example of the dreadful depravity of human nature as any that ever stained the criminal annals of the county.

Although the motive for the murder was never publicly established, the *Western Flying Post* suggested that as James Marsh was to have married the week after the murder was committed, it was supposed that he meant to get the necessary cash by robbing and killing Robert Parsons.

# FRAUDSTERS

From the *Western Flying Post* of 10 February 1857:

Elizabeth Darwent was brought up on a charge of endeavouring to obtain money by false pretences. It appeared that she went to the shop of Mr Tarrant in Middle Street, Yeovil, and offered a ring which she stated to be of gold, showing a fictitious mark in it, to prove the statement. She asked 3s.6d. for it. Mr Tarrant did not purchase it, but had the ring shown to Mr Cox, jeweller, who discovered that it was a brazen one, not worth more than about 3d. Information was given to the police and the prisoner was taken into custody. She now stated that she bought the ring as jeweller's gold and gave 9s.6d. for it. The Bench permitted her to be discharged, on promising to leave the town.

There was a General Election in the summer of 1895, and on Sunday 14 July, Dr James Russell presented himself at the Duke of Cornwall Inn, Stoke sub Hamdon, and took a room. He was a pleasant enough fellow, and he told the landlady, Mrs Chant, that he had a practice in a village in Berkshire and was the nephew of Sir Charles Russell, MP. Dr Russell explained that he was canvassing for Mr Turner, the Conservative candidate, and hired the landlady's horse and trap to travel around the villages; he also borrowed five shillings. The following Thursday, the 19th, the doctor took breakfast, ordered dinner for 5.30pm and walked out never to return, leaving an unpaid bill of £2.9s.6d. (a couple of weeks' pay for a skilled man).

On Friday afternoon, 19 July, a Dr James Russell arrived at the Mudford Inn and ordered tea. He informed the landlord, George Dimond, that he had been sent to Mudford by Mr Brown, the Conservative election agent in Yeovil, to make an independent canvass for Mr Turner. The doctor went on to say that he was a man of means, with an income of several thousand pounds a year, and had left a coach and four horses at Stoke waiting for election day, when they would be placed at the disposal of the Conservative candidate. During the evening Dr Russell ordered three rounds of beer for himself and fellow drinkers and smoked a threepenny cigar and enjoyed a glass of whisky. He stayed overnight and had Saturday breakfast. After spending some time with the landlord in the yard discussing pigs and his own farm of 90 acres, Dr Russell returned to the parlour where he sat down, put up his feet, ordered a glass of beer, smoked a cigar and then enjoyed a hearty lunch and another beer. By now, landlord Dimond was becoming a little suspicious of his guest who had arrived without any luggage and, although he had said the trunk was on its way from Yeovil, nothing had turned up. Finally, the landlord asked for payment for the food and drink from the bar but the doctor became quite incensed, stating that he never paid any bill until he left. He also refused to pay a deposit of a sovereign as a sign of good faith and went out into the village street where he met Mr John Golledge, the Yeovil Poor Law Union Relieving Officer. Dr Russell introduced himself and both men adjourned to the inn for drinks, paid for by Mr Golledge. The doctor then accompanied his newfound acquaintance on a drive around Marston Magna, Rimpton and Chilton Cantelo, and on returning to the Mudford Inn, he was driven to Yeovil, leaving his bill unpaid.

A furious George Dimond hurried to Yeovil to report to the police and, establishing that Dr Russell had no connection with the Conservative candidate or his agent, a warrant was issued for the doctor's arrest. The wanted man was spotted going into the Conservative Hall in Princes Street and arrested by Superintendent Self.

Dr James Russell, described as a well-dressed young man appeared in Yeovil Police Court on Monday 22 July, charged with obtaining food and lodging by false pretences. One of the witnesses was Mr John Farley, a Yeovil corn merchant, who stated that on 13 July the prisoner had called at his shop claiming to be the grandson of Mr George Sanger the circus proprietor, and ordered goods and feed for the circus which he said would be coming to the town the following Thursday. A suspicious Mr Farley refused to do business and suggested that he look elsewhere. The court was told that other charges were being considered and there were warrants out for the prisoner in Dorset; he was remanded in custody until Tuesday week.

On 30 July, Francis Bestes Devine, alias Dr James Russell, reappeared in court charged with obtaining food, lodging and money by false pretences at Mudford and Stoke sub Hamdon.

John Devine, an inspector in the Metropolitan Police, appeared and stated that the prisoner was his brother whom he had last seen in 1892 following his discharge from the Army. He was no doctor and to Mr Devine's knowledge had no occupation.

Francis Devine was sent for trial at the October Quarter Sessions where he was found guilty and sentenced to six months' hard labour.

In May 1922, following a trial which had gripped the nation's imagination, Ronald True was found guilty of the murder of a better class prostitute, Gertrude Yates, alias Olive Young, and despite strong pleas that he was insane, True was sentenced to death. However, he was reprieved and sent to Broadmoor where he died in 1951. The *Western Gazette* of 10 March 1922, when Ronald True was first arrested, reported that:

> True is said at one time during the war to have been engaged at the Westland Aircraft Works at Yeovil. When the works took in hand the construction of the famous D.H. series of aeroplanes, True came to Yeovil as test pilot, the aerodrome then being ready for testing the machines before delivery, the sea-planes previously constructed there being packed and sent away for test. It was said that his limping gait was the result of a crash whilst on active service, and he was looked upon as a daredevil airman, and enjoyed a certain amount of local hero-worship at a time when fighting aeroplanes were a novelty in the air in the Yeovil neighbourhood. After a series of minor crashes he left Yeovil and it was understood that he had gone to America.

Lieutenant General Anthony Edward Shaw, an elderly bachelor, was an impressive man in his early sixties, and his proposed marriage to the Yeovil widow, with whom he lodged, was accepted. He was a good talker and his military record impressive. So the credit of £2.11s. the General obtained from Templeman's shop in Yeovil, and the £10 from the Midland Bank was no problem; neither was the £140 from the Yeovil widow.

However, Lieutenant General Anthony Edward Shaw, was no gentleman. In fact he was Ernest Raymond Harper, of no fixed address, when he appeared before the Salisbury Quarter Sessions in April 1953, pleading guilty to a series of false pretences in Wiltshire and Somerset, including the widow's £140, and asked for a string of similar offences in Yeovil and Crewkerne to be taken into consideration. It was also divulged that the prisoner, as well as masquerading as a captain, major general and lieutenant general, had also styled himself Lawrence of Arabia. When challenged that Lawrence of Arabia had been killed in a motorcycle crash, Harper had strenuously argued that he was Lawrence and the man killed had been his double! It was also disclosed that Harper had 11 previous convictions since 1931, including three cases of bigamy, and had spent some twelve years in prison. After a remand for a medical examination, which concluded that the prisoner was perfectly sane, the sixty-two-year-old rogue was sentenced to seven years' preventive detention.

# A DEATH FROM NEGLECT

Late in the bitterly cold evening of Monday 8 January 1838, Mr William Porter's servant, Caroline Evans, answered the door and was sure the vagrant she saw swaying in the winter gloom was drunk. Mr Porter was Secretary of the Yeovil Mendicant Society, formed to give assistance to vagrants and other unfortunates passing through the town. To Caroline Evans this was just one more seeking help so she went to get her employer. Believing the dishevelled figure to be intoxicated, Mr Porter told the man to go away and shut the door; the society did not help drunken vagrants. About ten minutes later Caroline Evans again answered the bell and this time she found John Slade, the Borough Constable, standing at the door accompanied by the man who had just been refused assistance. On the appearance of Mr Porter, the constable asked what he should with the vagrant and was told to take him in charge, and the door closed once again on the cold January evening. Two days later, Caroline Evans identified the corpse lying in the watch-house as the vagrant who had called on the previous Monday evening, and three months later she was in the witness box at the Somerset Assizes at the trial of Watchmen George Hill and James Beare who stood charged with the manslaughter of a person unknown by neglect on 8 January previous.

In 1838 law enforcement within the boundaries of Yeovil was carried out by two unpaid Borough Constables, ancient offices chosen annually at the Court Leet, and under the Yeovil Improvement Act of 1830, a Superintendent (also known as the Beadle) and four part-time watchmen employed by the Town Commissioners. A watch-house was opened in George Court (roughly the site of the Borough Arcade which runs between High Street and South Street), the Superintendent patrolling the town during the daytime and two watchmen patrolling at night between the hours of 10pm and 6am. The watchmen wore dark brown greatcoats with scarlet collars bearing their numbers in white, leather hats, and each carried a rattle, stave and cutlass. The records of the Town Commissioners show that on occasion the watchmen were not the most reliable of public servants!

On 18 January 1838, George Hill and James Beare were committed to Ilchester Gaol to await trial, and we have a brief glimpse of the two men. Hill is described as being thirty-four years old, 5 feet 9 inches tall and of stout build with a round pock-marked face, by trade a shoemaker and married with eight children. Beare, a carpenter, was forty-seven, 6 feet tall and also of stout build but with a long face bearing scars on the right cheek; he was married with 11 children.

The trial, before Lord Denman, opened in Taunton on 6 April 1838 with Caroline Evans describing the events at the house of Mr Porter on 8 January. The next witness was John Slade, the Borough Constable. who recalled finding a man lying in the road near Mr Porter's house, and he had at first thought him to be intoxicated. After helping the man to his feet he told Slade that he had been refused assistance and the witness had then gone back to Mr Porter's house to ask what had happened. Mr Porter explained that as the man was drunk he had refused relief, and suggested that Slade take the vagrant into charge for the night. Finding that the man had no money for a bed, the witness took him to the watch-house for a few hours out of the bitter cold. Asked why he appeared to be intoxicated, the vagrant replied that he was a cripple, and had drunk nothing for some time. The watch-house was dark and empty when Slade arrived and after sitting the man on a bench in the far corner he left, saying that someone would come back and light the fire. He then shut the door but did not lock it as it could not be opened from the inside. Both the Borough Constables and the watchmen used the watch-house as a lock-up, but the Constables did not have the keys. Slade stated that he had then gone to George Hill's house in George Court, to tell the watchman what he had done. Hill was out on duty but his partner, Watchman Beare, walked past and the witness told him that he had put a man in the watch-house, not as a prisoner but as a place of refuge, and asked him to let the vagrant go the next morning. Beare replied that he would and Slade went on his way. Later in the evening the witness saw Watchman Hill and told him about the man put in the watch-house, and asked for his release the next morning. On Wednesday evening the witness stated that he had heard that someone had just been found dead in the watch-house, and on checking found that it was the vagrant he had left there two days before. Slade understood that George Hill had been out of town all day Tuesday but did not know where Beare was.

The next witness was Ann Hellier, who stated that she lived in George Court and had seen the Borough Constable put the man in the watch-house, and heard James Beare say that he would take care of him.

Humphrey Jeanes lived opposite the watch-house, and recalled hearing groans coming from the building early on Wednesday morning. However, he did not go to investigate because he often heard such noises coming from it.

John Lugg, son of Watchman Charles Lugg, told of going to the watch-house at about seven o'clock on Wednesday evening to light the fire for his father who would be going on duty later in the evening. The door was fastened and once inside young Lugg saw something lying on the floor, but as he had forgotten his candle, he went on to chapel. The boy returned with a light at about a quarter to ten and saw a man lying on the floor; he then ran to get his father.

Charles Lugg testified that he had been on duty at the watch-house on Sunday night 7 January, and George Hill and James Beare were on duty on the Monday and Tuesday nights. The weather had been very cold and only about £2 a year was allowed for the watch-house fire. When on duty the watchmen were instructed to visit the watch-house regularly and it was his practice to do so. The witness stated that he had sent his son to start the fire for the Wednesday night patrol and on finding the body he had gone to tell George Hill, whom he found to be rather intoxicated.

Surgeon William Tomkins stated that he was one of the Town Commissioners, and on being notified of the death by Watchmen Hill and Lugg, he had gone to see the body. He had no doubt that the vagrant had not eaten for over forty-eight hours, and had died from want, starvation and cold. Mr Tomkins stated that he found some bread and cheese in the deceased's pocket but considered that he was too ill to eat it. If the man had been ill when he was put in the watch-house, the cold could have accelerated his death, but if food and warmth had been given, he might have lived. The surgeon confirmed that the dead man had not drunk alcohol for some considerable time, and Mr Porter must have been mistaken if he thought the deceased was drunk. Mr John Batten, Clerk to the Commissioners, presented the appointments of the two watchmen in which their duties were set out and requiring attendance at the watch-house

At the conclusion of the trial, the Judge, Lord Denman, summed up the evidence and pointed out to the jury that between 8 and 9 January, Hill and Beare had charge of the watchhouse, they had been informed that an unknown weak and sick man had been put in it and had undertaken to look after him. However, they had at no time visited the watch-house, and had left the deceased without food, drink or warmth and as a result of this neglect the man had died. It was for the jury to decide whether the evidence laid before them proved to their satisfaction that the two prisoners, or either of them, were the cause of the death of the unfortunate man.

The jury found George Hill and James Beare guilty of manslaughter by neglect, but the Judge deferred the sentence for consultation with twelve Judges as he believed this to be a novel case. As the law stood in 1838 there was no right of appeal, but the sentence could be deferred and decided at a later date by the trial Judge after consultation with his fellow Judges.

On 1 May 1838 both prisoners were released having entered into their own recognisance to appear to receive judgement if called upon.

On 12 January 1838 'A Man (found dead in the watchhouse)' was buried in St John's churchyard.

# GORE LANGTON'S OLD TROUSERS, AND OTHER SURPRISING STORIES

In January 1870, John Churchill, yeoman, was summonsed by Edward Mear for assault. Edward Mear testified that John Churchill had insulted him at the Ashill Inn on 7 January by declaring that he, the complainant, was wearing a pair of Gore Langton's old trousers. He had replied that he was certainly not, but he would be proud to wear the trousers of such a fine man. Edward Mear then retorted that John Churchill was wearing someone's old hat and was promptly punched in the mouth.

Witness Robert Binden, testified that John Churchill had shouted out that the complainant was wearing a pair of Gore Langton's old trousers, and he had told him that he should apologise for mentioning Mr Langton's name in such a way in a public house, as he was the best gentleman in Somerset. Edward Mear had responded by saying that the defendant had had a windfall as he was wearing someone's old hat; following which John Churchill hit Edward Mear in the mouth.

Thomas Vincent, the landlord of the Ashill Inn deposed that there had been bad feeling between the two men, and on the night in question, John Churchill had been quarrelsome.

In his defence, John Churchill stated that he had gone to the inn to carryout some business, and had heard Robert Binden boasting that he had lent someone £600 but had not asked for interest for five years. Edward Mear was also boasting about his money. John Churchill told the court that he had said that if he had so much money he had better pay the shilling he owed him. With that, Edward Mear had come over to him but he had only pushed him away and struck no blow.

The Magistrates were not impressed and fined John Churchill ten shillings with 17s.6d. costs.

And who was Gore Langton? William Henry Powell Gore Langton Esq., of Hatch Court, Hatch Beauchamp, was one of the two local Members of Parliament, and a Justice of the Peace, but why wearing his old trousers could cause such offence is probably lost in the mists of time.

In August 1814, the *Taunton Courier* reported that Ann Lansdown, a labouring woman from Bath, had been committed to Ilchester Gaol charged with stealing a cambric muslin petticoat and a muslin-worked gown from Priscilla Staples of Widcombe. The gaol register describes the prisoner as being thirty-five years of age, 5 feet 4 inches tall, with brown hair, a fair complexion and a cut on her under-lip.

The *Taunton Courier* went on to disclose that Ann Lansdown had been born in Dorchester and married at the age of nineteen to George Lansdown, a sailor, and:

> from regard for her husband went, in disguise as a jolly boy, with him on board the *Levanter* transport in the expedition to Holland. She stood with her husband at the gun in an engagement. When on shore with the jolly boat, she was with 150 men, taken prisoner, and carried to Amsterdam; at the end of the month an exchange took place, and she again joined her husband in the *Levanter.* On going on board, she secretly conveyed some gin under her trousers, which being discovered by the master-at-arms, she was tried by court martial and sentenced to received two dozen lashes; but, on being stripped her sex was discovered, and, by order of Capt. Thompson, a woman was sent for on board with apparel for her; the greatest care was taken of her, and she was landed at Blackwall in about a fortnight after. She then went before the Queen, who gave her a written paper empowering her to receive ten guineas at Greenwich. Her husband was one of the eleven sailors who were hung for mutiny on the conclusion of the last peace.

Ann Lansdown was sentenced to six months for the offence, but after her release from Ilchester Gaol she disappears from the record.

In the summer of 1829, the son of the Langport Turnpike Trust toll keeper, encouraged by two farmer's boys, helped himself to some of the tolls so that the three could play 'pitch and toss' for half-crowns; large sums of cash in those days. When the lad's father discovered what had happened he was understandably furious, and after telling the farmer, the two men decided to administer some effective homespun justice, and the *Western Flying Post* described how they went about it:

The farmer conceiving that the imprisoning of the two young offenders among practised and hardened old ones would only plant more corruption more deeply in their minds, contented himself with threatening to send them instantly to gaol, unless they would agree to obey his orders; these were that they should tie each other up by turns to the turnpike gate, and flog each other with a good ground ash stick. The lads preferred this alternative to confinement in gaol, and belaboured each other in right earnest until the farmer was satisfied. It was now the toll keeper's turn, who tying up his son in the same manner, flogged him with such severity that the farmer thought proper to interfere on his behalf with his exasperated father. All the inhabitants of the neighbouring village, and several gentlemen travelling on the road, witnessed the administration of the wholesome discipline. There are thousands of instances like the above in which the infliction of sound corporal punishment would be far preferable to imprisonment, and deter youth from prosecuting a career which is sure to lead to an ignominious end.

In November 1900, an Ilminster butcher appeared before the Magistrates charged with furiously driving a horse and cart in Ilminster on the previous 26 September. He pleaded not guilty, but the local newspaper reported that during the whole of the proceedings the butcher continually interrupted with interjections and contradictions.

Police Sergeant Powell testified that at about eleven o'clock on the night in question he had been on duty in Silver Street and saw the defendant driving furiously towards him from the direction of Station Road. He estimated that the cart was travelling at about 14 miles an hour and he shouted at the defendant to slow down, but this was ignored and the defendant continued to drive furiously into East Street where he stopped. Sergeant Powell stated he had then spoken to the defendant, who in reply had used very bad language and a summons was issued for using threatening language, which the Magistrates then proceeded to hear.

Sergeant Powell stated that the butcher had threatened to beat his brains out and on being told to stop this bad language he had run off to the yard of his slaughterhouse where he had taken off his jacket and tried to get into his shop shouting, 'Give me a hatchet and I'll knock his brains out!' The sergeant said that fortunately the shop was locked because he feared the defendant would have carried out his threat if he had been able to get a hatchet. Sergeant Powell added that the defendant was under the influence of drink at the time.

At this point in the case, the butcher shouted out, 'I will have a sale and leave the town next week. I can't stand this, every week he is after me!'

Police Superintendent Jennings asked the Magistrates to bind the defendant over to keep the peace, and pointed out that he had threatened to buy a gun and shoot the sergeant's brains out; it was not the first time these threats had been made.

Colonel Blake, the Chairman of the Magistrates, reminded the defendant that he had been before the court before, and that it might be a good idea if he did sell up and leave the town.

For the furious driving the butcher was fined £1 and six shillings costs, for threatening the police sergeant, he was ordered to pay the eight shillings costs and bound over on his own surety of £10 to keep the peace for six months. On hearing the decision the defendant yelled, 'I wish to go the gaol', and was taken to the cells. However, he paid the fine and costs, and his brother stood surety for him.

In 1974, Jack Nicholson, Otis Young and Randy Quaid, starred in the film *The Last Detail,* often shown on television, which tells the story of a young US sailor convicted of theft. He is being escorted to a military prison by two veteran senior ratings, and on the way the three get to know each other, and the young prisoner is given a taste of life before being put behind bars. Truth can sometimes be stranger than fiction (or so they say), and over a century before the film was made, the *Western Flying Post* reported in September 1866 the following military frolic in Taunton:

Last week an escort from the Portland convict establishment indulged in a frolic, for which no doubt they have since suffered. It appears that a corporal and private of the 56th Regiment of Foot, stationed at Portland, were sent to this town to fetch a prisoner from the gaol. They were billeted at the Bristol Inn for the night, and on the morning obtained their prisoner. But instead of returning home by the eleven o'clock train, the attractions of East Reach, a low part of the town, drew them with the prisoner to that neighbourhood. They soon visited the public houses, and by the afternoon each man had quite enough to look after himself. In this state they all made a perambulation round the town, the novelty of the thing causing lots of followers. They thus continued till about seven in the evening, when they were taken into custody by a couple of sergeants of the Coldstream Guards and Royal Marines, and despatched to Portland the next morning.

# FIRE!!

Fire is an ever present menace, even at the beginning of the twenty-first century with all our sophisticated methods of warning and precaution. It was a greater menace in the past when so many buildings in the crowded towns and villages were built from timber and had thatched roofs. A fire could spread with disastrous consequences.

Yeovil suffered two severe fires in the past. In 1450, 117 houses were destroyed, and in July 1640, when Walter Whitcombe's house caught fire, the flames, fanned by a strong wind, destroyed 83 houses, scores of barns and outbuildings, and left over 6000 people homeless.

Needless to say, anyone caught deliberately starting a fire could expect and receive no mercy – arson was a hanging offence!

On a Saturday night in April 1790, fire broke out in Yeovil at the Greyhound Inn (the present Greyhound in South Street is a descendent on the same site), destroting the cellar and several outhouses. On the following Wednesday, a second fire was discovered in some more outbuildings, but with the help of the Sherborne fire engine, the fire was put out before it could spread to the inn itself. When a third fire broke out and gutted the next-door smithy owned by Thomas Garland, the landlord of the Greyhound, the suspicions of arson were confirmed, and nineteen-year-old Alexander Pearce, a servant at the inn, was arrested.

Alexander Pearce appeared at the Somerset Assizes in the following August and was found guilty of setting fire to the house and outbuildings of his master. He was sentenced to death and hanged, protesting his innocence, at Ilchester on 25 August 1790.

On Tuesday, 10 March 1863, three people lost their lives in a fearsome fire at the John Bull Inn, in the lower part of Yeovil's Middle Street.

At about three o'clock on the Tuesday morning, Walter Hurdle, a cheese factor, was shaken awake by his wife who shouted, 'For God's sake whats that!' and pointed to the bedroom window. Jumping out of bed and pulling up the window blind, Walter Hurdle was horrified to see flames leaping from the John Bull Inn on the other side of the street. Leaning out he shouted, 'Fire! Police! Fire!' for about five minutes before going down to see if he could help.

The following story emerged at the inquest into the burning to death of Mrs Gulliver, the wife of the landlord, and her young son and daughter.

The fire, which appeared to have broken out in the kitchen, had taken a firm hold and was burning fiercely before it was discovered by the landlord's eleven-year-old son Alfred, who woke his father and then Edward James, the ostler. The ostler slept in the room over the kitchen and flames were already licking around the door when he scrambled out of bed. Climbing out through the window, Edward James dropped into the yard below and, taking a ladder from the empty stable, propped it against the wall under the window. Smoke was pouring from the room and first to leave was the lodger, Richard Warr, who fell off the ladder but luckily only received slight bruising from his fall. Then came John Gulliver, who kept calling back for his son but no one followed.

A neighbour, Robert Hewlett, helped by John Bunn, broke open the doors to the yard of the John Bull, and rushing in met the distraught land-lord, who cried that his wife and family were trapped in the front bedroom. Tragically, Richard Hewlett and Constable William Parson's efforts to rescue the family through the bedroom window failed as they were driven back by the flames. An attempt by Richard Hewlett to get into the front bedroom through a second bedroom failed as flames burst through the communicating door, and he narrowly escaped death when the roof fell in just after he had climbed out.

The police and the volunteer fire brigade with their three engines, were soon on the scene, but all thoughts of saving the landlord's family and his inn had gone and it was now a question of containing the spread of the flames. Aided by a still night, the brigade saved the three adjoining cottages and by early morning the fire was out. The badly burnt remains of Mrs Gulliver and her two children were found in the charred shell of the inn

The cause of the fire which destroyed the John Bull Inn was never established, and the inquest jury returned a verdict of 'death by burning but by what means the fire originated there is no evidence.'

The fire in Mr Henry White's upholsterer's workshops in Union Street, Yeovil, broke out just after one o'clock on Monday afternoon on 23 May 1881. Feeding on the packing materials, dry wood and shavings, the fire soon took hold and within minutes smoke was billowing from the premises. However, the early arrival of the volunteer fire brigade, led by Lieutenant Damon, soon contained the fire to the ground floor and prevented its spread to adjoining buildings.

At about two o'clock when the blaze had been subdued, a ladder was put up to a first-floor window and Volunteer Fireman T.W.Vincent climbed up to inspect the extent of the damage. He smashed the smoke- blackened glass, pushed in the frame, and peered into the room. To his horror he picked out the form of a small child huddled by the wall under the window.

Reaching in, Fireman Vincent lifted the child, and to the cries of consternation from the watching crowd, carried it gently back down the ladder. The small victim was found to be dead, and quickly identified as Frederick White, the upholsterer's four-year-old son. Although the fire had seriously damaged the workshops, the boy had not been burnt, but had died from the effect of smoke. Frederick was carried to his home in Peter Street and his distraught parents, but people were asking why was he in the building and why did nobody know?

On Wednesday 25 May, the inquest into the death of young Frederick White opened in the Swan Inn, Park Street, before the Coroner, Dr Wybrants, and a 'respectable jury'. The first witness was Mr John Conway who said that he was employed by Mr White and knew the young deceased. Mr Conway stated that just before one o'clock on the day in question he had taken Frederick from the workshop to his home in Peter Street and left the child in the front passage of the house. He had then returned to the workshop and had left for his dinner at about ten minutes past one. The fire had broken after he had gone, and he had not seen Frederick return to the workshop. The witness went on to say that there had been a stray cat and her kittens in the room above the workshops and Frederick used to go there to play with them. Mr Conway suggested that the boy had gone back to see the kittens after he had taken him home.

Volunteer Fireman Vincent the next witness, stated that within five minutes of the call, all members of the brigade were on the spot. The flames had been so fierce that at first they could not get near the buildings, but within less than an hour the fire had been subdued sufficiently to enable a ladder to be put up. He had climbed up the ladder and after breaking the window had looked in to see if the floor was safe enough to allow him to enter the room. Fireman Vincent then described how he saw the boy lying on his back below the window, apparently quite dead but not burnt. He believed that when the fire had broken out, the boy had been in the room above the workshop, but running to the staircase he had found it blocked by flames, and had gone back into the room where he was found. The child was not tall enough to be seen through the window and had been suffocated by the thick smoke. In reply to a question from one of the jurors, Fireman Vincent did not know whether the front door of the building had been locked, but Mr Henry White, who was present, told the Jury that it was never locked during the day. The witness said that he had been the first fireman on the scene, and although people were saying that a boy was missing, he took this to mean one of Mr White's workshop boys who would have been able to make his way out of the building.

At this point, sensing criticism of the Fire Brigade, Mr W.N. Thring, the foreman of the jury, stated that he had been present at the fire, and he thought the members of the brigade did well.

Fireman Vincent continued with his evidence, and stated that had the brigade known that there was a child in the building, they would have played the hoses on the room concerned at the expense of the rest of the buildings, and taken the most strenuous efforts to get him out. They had only heard the vague rumour of a child being missing, but not who or where, and had not the remotest idea that there was anyone trapped in the blazing building. The fire was one of the fiercest he had seen in such a small space.

No more witnesses were called, and following his summing up, the Coroner said that there was only one verdict open to the jury, and that was 'accidentally smothered'. The jury commented that the contents of the building were very combustible, and the child must have fallen as soon as he got to the window. They were unanimous in returning a verdict of accidentally smothered.

Next door to Mr White's workshops was a private school run by Mr G.S. Stone, and which had been in danger from the fire. On 2 June 1881 the *Western Gazette* published the following letter from Mr Stone:

Will you allow me to correct a false report current in the town, concerning two country pupils who were in my schoolroom during the dinner hour on the day of the fire? It seems generally believed that three boys were locked in by way of punishment and when the fire broke out on the adjoining premises their lives were in jeopardy. Some also add that the door was broken open to liberate them before the key could be procured. The facts of the case are, however, that a couple of country pupils are allowed to stay in the room to take their dinner, by way of accommodation, as they had all asked for a half-holiday (instead of the following Wednesday) to attend the rifle battalion drill in Barwick Park, and they were furnished with the key to liberate them-selves when they chose, but were requested to leave it at my house on their way to the park. They tell me that they had taken their exit from the school before any alarm of fire took place, and were on their way to deliver the key before they heard of it. The statements also prove that the boy one of the spectators saw at one of the schoolroom windows could not have been either of those in question, but must have been one of the solicited or unsolicited helpers in the removal of the furniture of the room after the door had been broken open by the fire brigade, before my arrival.

# THE WIDCOMBE BRIDGE DISASTER

The Bath & West of England Society and Southern Counties Association's five-day annual show was held at different venues each year, and in 1877 it opened in Bath, for the first time in thirteen years, on Monday 4 June to fine summer weather; the following day was just as sunny, and the blue skies of Wednesday morning the 6th, heralded another beautiful summer day. The third day of the show usually attracted the largest number of excursionists and on this fine Wednesday, the numbers arriving at Bath Railway Station from all parts of the western counties, was larger than in previous years.

At 10.54am on the Wednesday morning, an excursion train from Weymouth, calling at all stations, arrived with some 900 passengers at Bath and the majority were bound for the showground on the opposite side of the River Avon. Behind the station, a footbridge crossed the river to Widcombe and a notice was displayed on the station side announcing 'Nearest way to the Show Field – Toll one halfpenny'. Taking heed of the notice, hundreds of the newly arrived visitors made their way onto the bridge and within a short time several hundred people were standing on it waiting to pass through the toll gate at the opposite end where the collector was overwhelmed by the volume of customers. The fifteen-year-old footbridge was described as a wooden-trussed bow-string girder bridge built of wood and iron, some 9 feet wide and with a single span about 100 feet long some 30 feet above the River Avon.

Suddenly there was a terrible crack as the bridge broke in the middle, and then at each end, and fell with its human cargo into the river with some victims being thrown onto the tow path on the Widcombe side. An eyewitness described the scene:

'I saw them go down, but I wish I hadn't. For Good God! – it was fearful! I stood upon the bank on the opposite side of the river looking out for a friend whom I expected to arrive. The bridge was densely covered with a good-tempered and well-dressed crowd of excursionists, full of jest and humour. There was a block on account of some dispute between one of the passengers and the toll-collector, and during the dispute the bridge was seen to rock and the timbers were heard to creak. We on the embankment – about 30 feet below the level of the bridge – scarcely had time to give a warning of danger when lo! an indescribable crash, a chorus of heart rending terrible shrieks – and a plunging, struggling mass was hurled headlong into the water and upon the stone towing path by the side of the river.

Almost immediately rescuers were on the scene with rafts and boats plucking the scores of struggling people from the water, whilst others rendered first aid on the tow path and river bank. A local surgeon opened his nearby house to receive the more seriously injured where they were treated before being rushed to the Bath General Hospital. Although several hundred people had fallen with the bridge, the number of fatalities was thankfully small, some nine in all, but over 80 were injured, of which at least 50 were considered serious.

Many were the narrow escapes and acts of bravery. A Mr Burt from Yeovil, went onto the bridge but suddenly remembering he had left something behind at the railway station, went back to fetch it, and had scarcely put his feet off the bridge, when the fatal crash occurred. Nine people from Norton sub Hamdon were on the bridge when it fell and they all plunged into the river. Miraculously, they survived, although all but one received light to severe injuries. Mr Stay, a dairyman from Hinton St George, found himself trapped underwater but somehow struggled to the surface and was able to clamber up a rescue ladder.

Two brothers from Yetminster in Dorset, had not seen each other for nearly three years when they unexpectedly met in the crowd on the bridge. They described how they had just shaken hands when there was a creak, a strain and a huge crash, and the brothers pitched side by side into the river. One recalled how people scrambled over him as he struggled in the water, and he feared that he would be drowned. Despite his coat being torn to pieces in the mêlée, the Yetminster man managed to reach safety and was reunited with his brother. 'I thought that meeting Dick in this way after three years was one of the most extraordinary incidents in connection with the accident,' he exclaimed to a local journalist.

George Andress, a cooper from Beaminster, was about half-way across the bridge when it broke, but managed to keep his head above water by clinging to some wreckage and then scrambling up a rescue ladder. Trent farmer George Garrett had fallen into a mass of people and described how all around him they were fighting and struggling, each for themselves. Women were grasping each other by the hair and screaming. The farmer managed to grab hold of a piece of wood and held on for dear life until he was pulled aboard one of the rescue boats.

Edward Mitchell from Mere in Wiltshire, was waiting patiently on the bridge with his two sons and as he went down into the river he saw a man within a few feet of him killed by a severe blow to his head. After spending nearly half an hour in the water, Edward Mitchell was pulled out by rescuers in a boat. Both his sons survived and one had rescued a baby by diving under the water to rescue the infant and placing it in one of the boats.

As the news of the disaster flashed down the telegraphs on the main line from Bath to Weymouth and out to the branches, local people waited anxiously at the stations and halts for the return of their loved ones and friends. During the evening there were many emotional scenes as the special train arrived at each station from which so many had set off that morning looking for an enjoyable day out at the show.

On Friday, two days after the tragedy, General Ulysses S. Grant, ex-President of the United States of America visited Bath, and in his address to the Mayor and assembled citizens, expressed his deep sorrow at the great catastrophe which occurred the day before yesterday.

The death toll of nine, miraculously low bearing in mind the large number of people involved, was all Somerset and Dorset folk:

John Thorne, Charminster
Edward Linton, Sutton, near Evercreech
Andrew Harford, Weymouth
Emily Harford, Weymouth
John Gifford Male, East Chinnock, near Crewkerne
James Ford, Beerhacket, near Sherborne
Sarah Jane Gibbs, Sutton, near Evercreech
John Milborne, Yeovil
Mary Haines, Ilchester, near Yeovil

The lengthy inquest into the deaths resulted in the owners of the Widcombe Bridge being charged with manslaughter on grounds of culpable negligence, but when the case came for trial at the Somerset Assizes, the Grand Jury found there was insufficient evidence to proceed, and the defendants were discharged. The bridge was rebuilt in 1877 and still spans the River Avon.

# THE STONING OF A SCHOOLMASTER

Mrs Yeandle's afternoon rest in her sittingroom at 13 Market Street, Yeovil, was rudely interrupted by the sound of a mob of boys and girls approaching from the direction of Reckleford, and she became alarmed when they stopped outside her house and began shouting and chanting. Going out to investigate, she was just in time to see her lodger, Charles Hemmings, an assistant teacher at Reckleford School, run into the backway to the house and slam the door shut in the face of a pursuing mob of children.

The events of Thursday afternoon, 1 December 1881, would be recounted before the Borough Magistrates a few days later when two boys, William Hann and Frederick Day, both from Goar Knap, were summonsed for assaulting Charles Hemmings.

Mr William Marsh, prosecuting, stated that the complainant, Mr Hemmings, was a certificated teacher at the Reckleford Board School, and was under notice to leave. He would not go into the reason why Mr Hemmings was leaving, except to say that there was a certain amount of ill-feeling between the complainant and the Headmaster, Mr Robert Higham. After the school closed on 1 December, Mr Hemmings left as usual but was then pursued to his lodgings by about 100 boys and girls, including the two defendants, who called after him 'Sneak', 'Dead Master', 'got the sack', and other objectionable names, and he was pelted with stones and other missiles, including marbles. Mr Marsh stated that there was some evidence to indicate that the children had been incited to mob the complainant who had been injured by the stones and missiles.

The first witness was Mrs Yeandle, who described the events and believed that Mr Hemmings had narrowly escaped with his life. The mob had shouted, 'Get in after 'un, we'll horsewhip 'un, get in after 'un.' She had heard someone tell the children to go home but they had shouted, 'We bain't going – master told us to do it.' However, Mrs Yeandle could not recognise Hann and Day as being part of the mob. Doctor Colmer was called and Mr Hemmings was helped to bed.

Mr Charles Hemmings now took the stand and told how he had been pursued by the mob of children, and the two defendants were the ringleaders. He had always been on good terms with the children and alleged that the Headmaster had incited them to mob him.

Mrs Blake, another resident of Market Street, testified to the actions of the mob, but she had not seen the two defendants in the crowd.

Little Mary Foan said that she had seen the two boys throw stones at the teacher and heard them call out 'Sneak'.

Mr Harry Edwards, an assistant teacher at the Huish School and a friend of the complainant, stated that he had come to visit his friend and saw the crowd of boys and girls milling around outside No. 13 Market Street, but apart from much shouting, he had seen no stones thrown. When he enquired of the reason for this misbehaviour, the children had shouted back that they had been told to throw stones at Mr Hemmings. On calling for a policeman, one of the children had shouted, 'We don't care for the policeman, master told us to do it.'

Several children were called but all testified that they had seen stones thrown and heard names called, but none had seen the two defendants throw any missile.

The Magistrates gave William Hann the benefit of the doubt and dismissed the summons, but found Frederick Day guilty and fined him one shilling with no costs.

So what was the story behind the assault on Charles Hemmings and the allegation that the Headmaster had incited his pupils to attack him?

In 1881, elementary education for children between five and thirteen years, had been compulsory for just over ten years, and to ensure national standards, the Government made grants to the local School Boards and carried out annual inspections by HM Inspectors of Schools. Grants depended on the required standards being achieved in work, examinations and attendance; the qualified teaching staff were also concerned to have a favourable HM Inspectors' report on their Teacher's Certificate.

The allegations of incitement were investigated by the Yeovil School Board and it seems that the trouble originated in the poor keeping of the attendance registers at the Reckleford School. This had led to considerable friction between the Headmaster, Robert Higham and Charles Hemmings, the assistant teacher, who accused each other of incompetence and the suggested falsification and alteration of the registers. As both teacher's future careers and the Government grant could depend upon a good Inspectors' report, the situation was naturally somewhat fraught, to say the least.

Charles Hemmings accused his Headmaster of inciting the children to attack him, which was vigorously denied, and as no independent witness could be found, the School Board took no action. However, the question of the registers was the subject of concern, not only to the Yeovil School Board, but to the Department of Education, who after making inquiries, ordered that the year's grant for the Reckleford School be reduced by £23.12s.0d. for careless registration. The Headmaster accepted responsibility and reimbursed the School Board from his salary. In accepting payment the Board considered that 'he was not the only culpable person'.

# DANGEROUS ENGINES OF DESTRUCTION

The Golden Jubilee of King George III would be celebrated with a bang by the local volunteers at Galhampton, near Castle Cary, on 25 October 1809. The volunteers commanded by Colonel Woodforde, had placed a battery of cannon near Galhampton House in order to fire salutes to the monarch on entering the fiftieth year of his reign. The volunteers were not to be denied the Jubilee rejoicings, and were attending a public dinner in Castle Cary, together with the other festivities in the town. Captain John Burge had been given responsibility for the care of the battery, and had left Thomas Millard, a member of his Company, together with another Volunteer, in charge of the guns.

No officer or NCO was left to supervise the two volunteers, and it would seem that they became bored, and idle fingers can make mischief. Thomas Millard decided to light the touch-hole of one of the cannon as a jolly jape. However, the gun did not fire, and so Millard took a ramrod and standing in front of the muzzle, thrust it down the barrel whilst the touch-hole was still smouldering. The result was a foregone conclusion because the cannon immediately discharged and the unfortunate but foolish Thomas Millard, busily pushing the ram rod down the barrel was blown to pieces. The remains of poor Volunteer Millard, some of which had been propelled for some distance, were collected up, and what was left of the twenty-four-year-old deceased were buried in the parish churchyard on 29 October 1809

'Never, never, let your gun pointed be at anyone' begins the exhortation drummed into the heads of generations of recruits to Her Majesty's Armed Forces by gunnery instructors when firearms are first handed out and they are taught how to use them. As exhortations go this was, and continues to be, an extremely sensible one and perhaps if it had been given to some young boys nearly 200 years ago, an awful tragedy could have been avoided.

The *Western Flying Post* reported on the 25 August 1817, that an inquest had been held at Sutton Montis into the death of nine-year-old Eliza Grove who on the 16th of that month had been killed by her eleven-year-old uncle. The *Flying Post* reported that it appeared the boy had been keeping birds off the corn and had been entrusted with a gun but without flint or powder. After leaving the field, between eight and nine o'clock in the evening, he had met another boy, who also had a gun, and the two guns were placed side by side whilst the boys were learning to read. On parting in the dusk, the boy picked up his friend's gun by mistake and not knowing it was loaded with lead shot. The newspaper went on to record that the boy:

> On entering the house where he and the deceased lived, he levelled gun at the girl saying, 'Eliza, I'll shoot thee,' and immediately the contents were lodged in the neck of the unfortunate girl. Verdict: 'chance medley of circumstances.'

The *Western Flying Post* commented:

> We cannot refrain from adding, that it is much to be lamented that such engines of destruction should be put into the hands of such boys.

Even in the hands of experienced people, guns can be extremely dangerous to the handler as happened in Chard just before Christmas in 1887 when forty-one-year-old William Churchill accidentally shot himself.

The inquest into William Churchill's death was held in the Ship Inn. His wife Anne recalled that he had got up at about 5.20am on Wednesday 21 December and had gone downstairs carrying his gun. A few minutes later there was the sound of a shot, followed by a cry from William 'The gun has gone off and knocked me! Oh Nance, I think it's a bad job!' Rushing downstairs Ann Churchill saw to her horror William lying on the floor with blood pumping from a gaping wound in his thigh. As she tried to comfort her stricken husband, he moaned, 'I'm dead', and at this, the terrified woman ran to summon her next-door neighbour, Charles Cornelius. Although they tried their best, there was nothing Ann or Charles Cornelius could do to stem the flow of blood from William's main artery and he died before medical assistance could be brought. No one could establish how William Churchill came to shoot himself but it was accepted as being accidental, and the inquest jury returned a verdict to this effect.

It goes without saying guns are very dangerous 'engines of destruction'.

# A SUPPOSED CASE OF POISONING

In the year 1400 work began on the new church for the flourishing town of Chard, and in 1445, St Mary's was finally completed; it has remained little changed in appearance during the subsequent five and a half centuries. Internally, more has been altered in those intervening years, but there still remains the feeling of space and peace away from the bustle of modern Chard. There are some fine memorials in the church and one of the most impressive is high on the wall of the north chapel which shows the carved and painted figures of William Brewer, a local 'phisitian', who died in 1618, his wife Deanes, and their 11 children six boys and five girls.

Today the well-kept churchyard of St Mary's is a pleasant haven between busy roads, but on a dark Wednesday evening in November 1851 there was the sound of digging from the churchyard and a small group with lanterns clustered around a newly opened grave; outside the churchyard a small crowd watched the strange proceedings. The soil and mud was scraped from the lid and the coffin was slowly lifted from the grave in which it had lain for the past two and a half years.

In the late autumn of 1851, it was being whispered in Chard, that a twenty-four-year-old labourer named Samuel Rice, who had died over two years before, had been poisoned by his wife and something should be done about it! As the rumours grew, so did the excitement and finally the Vicar and churchwardens of St Mary's presented the Coroner with a formal request to hold 'an inquest upon the body of Samuel John Rice, who died in the month of May 1849 and lies buried in the churchyard of this parish, there being strong suspicion that he came to his death by unfair means'.

The Coroner ordered the corpse to be exhumed on 12 November, and the following day a 'respectable jury' was empanelled to enquire into the cause of death. The jury met in the Town Hall and 'determined that the poor fellow's remains – which consisted merely of putrid matter and bones – should be examined and tested by Mr R.W. Spicer, surgeon, who was directed (could he detect the least trace of any poisonous substance) to forward the remains to Mr Herepath for analyzation'. Mr William Herepath was one of the foremost chemists of the day and had gained a formidable reputation in the criminal courts in cases of poisoning. The inquest was adjourned to 20 November when the first witness, Mrs Elizabeth Symonds, testified that she had known Samuel Rice since he was a child and he had always been 'asthmatical' and occasionally very ill. She had been with him when he died, leaving a widow and an eleven-month-old child. Samuel had been taken ill on the Tuesday after Good Friday complaining of a great pain in his stomach and Mr Ware, the surgeon, had been called. Mrs Symonds went on to say that during this last illness she had never heard Samuel once complain about his treatment. In reply to a question from the Coroner, the witness said that Mrs Rice had always appeared very kind to her husband.

William Hill testified that he had lived 'under the same roof as the deceased who he had known from a boy. The deceased's health was very bad and he suffered from asthma.' During the weeks that he had been ill Samuel had complained about a pain in his stomach and had a very nasty cough after which he was often sick. Samuel's wife was always very kind and the couple 'used to play about in the garden like two children'. William Hill caused some laughter when he described the couple as 'resembling turtle doves'.

Mrs Sarah Hill followed her husband into the witness box and corroborated his evidence, adding that Samuel Rice was often sick after taking any kind of food. She believed that his wife had 'never a thought of injuring her husband, more than I had mine'. When the Coroner commented, 'We don't know what you would do to your husband,' Sarah Hill retorted, 'True sir, but I should never like to hurt him!'

The next witness was Samuel Ware, the surgeon, who stated that he had known Samuel Rice from his birth and had attended him professionally for many years. His patient had suffered from asthma and had been ill for some six weeks before the surgeon had been called in on the 22 April. Mr Ware stated that the 'deceased was suffering from inflammation of the bowels', and this condition had been the cause of his natural death. The surgeon added that Mrs Rice had always seemed very kind and during her husband's last illness had seemed very depressed and anxious about his condition.

The last witness was Mr R.W. Spicer, the surgeon who had examined the remains. He stated that the body was very decomposed but his tests had revealed no traces of arsenic or any other poison. The surgeon agreed with his colleague, Mr Ware, that death was 'the natural result of chronic inflammation of the bowels'.

Following Mr Spicer's evidence, the jury quickly returned the verdict that Samuel Rice had died from natural causes and 'he had experienced every kindness from his wife'.

Why did the rumours start two and a half years after Samuel's death – was it something his widow said or did, or was there some maliciousness, the cause of which is lost in the years which have passed?

# GILES HUTCHINGS ESCAPES

On the night of 16 November 1876, the East Coker policeman, Nathaniel Cox, was killed and his colleague, Constable Henry Stacey of West Coker, severely beaten in a fight with a gang of local poachers. A West Coker villain, Charles Baker, was quickly taken into custody but the other wanted men, who came from Hardington Mandeville, George Hutchings and his sons, Giles and Peter, went into hiding and were not arrested until early in January 1877.

The following March all four appeared at the Somerset Assizes charged with the murder of Nathaniel Cox, but because the two policemen were known to have had a few drinks during that last patrol, and the impossibility of establishing who struck the fatal blows, the jury returned verdicts of 'guilty of manslaughter'. The three Hutchings and George Baker were each sentenced to twenty-four years' penal servitude, but following a statement by Baker that George Hutchings had not been involved, the old man was granted a Free Pardon; however, he died in gaol before he was released.

One year later at about ten o'clock in the morning of 30 April 1878, Giles Hutchings escaped from a gang working on the extension to the Chatham Dockyard. It was reported that:

> his escape was very cleverly effected, as there were several armed warders attached to the gang to which he belonged. He was engaged in wheeling a barrow containing bricks, taking his turn with the other convicts. He had wheeled several barrows in this manner but when it came to his turn again he was missing. An alarm was at once raised and all the convicts who engaged in the neighbourhood, numbering about 1000, were taken back to prison, and a thorough search was instituted. It is believed that his escape was witnessed by other convicts but they would not tell. He has given almost more trouble than any other convict at the prison and attempted to elude the vigilance of his keepers on Saturday, but was detected. Armed warders are still searching the district for him. Some think that, as he has not been seen, he might have lost his life in attempting the River Medway; but the general belief is that he is still hiding because the district is a very woody one.

There were rumours that Giles Hutchings had been seen in the Hardington area and had then gone to America, but as the months passed without his recapture, most people began to believe that he had drowned.

Three and a half years later a man fitting Giles Hutchings description was found living in a small cottage outside the village of Niton on the south coast of the Isle of Wight. Despite protesting that he was not Hutchings, the man was taken into custody on suspicion of being an escaped convict but on the way to Newport he made a break for freedom. After a long chase over streams and fields the suspect was recaptured and on reaching Newport police station the 'delicate looking fellow, about thirty-six years of age, with flowing beard and bilious complexion' was identified as being Giles Hutchings from the description on the wanted posters.

Formal identification was given by several warders from Chatham Prison, and Giles Hutchings was taken under close guard to Pentonville to serve out the full term of twenty-four years' penal servitude.

It was reported that for most of his time on the run Giles Hutchings had adopted the name of Williams and had lived the quiet life of a labourer, raising pigs and fowls and tending his small cottage garden. He had also worked for a time as a bricklayer's labourer on the building of the new police station and cells in Newport!

# THE NOTORIOUS MAGGS AND SPARROW

A little after nine o'clock on the morning of Wednesday 24 September 1851, John Watts and his wife Leah set out from Bottle's Farm, at West Woodland, to walk the three miles to Frome market. Left behind to mind the farm was their fourteen-year-old daughter Sarah. The couple returned at about four o'clock that afternoon to find Sarah lying dead in the dairy room amongst smashed basins and the contents of an upturned whey tub; she had been battered, raped and strangled.

Sergeant Henry Smith, of the London Metropolitan Detective Office, was bought down to lead the investigation, but no one had witnessed the murder and the only clue was a silk handkerchief found on the farmhouse kitchen table. James Watts denied the rumours that he had kept the large sum of £250 in the house. The farmhouse had been ransacked: a watch, the farmer's coat and waistcoat, and his wife's shawl were missing, the clothing was being discovered in a nearby field. Several local men who had been seen in the vicinity during the morning and afternoon of 24 September, including an uncle of the murdered girl, were questioned and released. The official reward of £50 for the arrest and conviction of the killer or killers, was increased to £100, by the Marchioness of Bath, who also visited the bereaved parents.

Within a matter days, however, there were three names in the frame of prime suspects. Forty-six- year-old William Maggs, a convicted thief, William Sparrow, a thirty-year-old twice-convicted felon, and Robert Hurd, aged thirty-seven, a pickpocket and prizefighter going by the name of 'Frome Bob'. The *Western Flying Post* reported the the three villains had formed a gang 'which had infested the neighbourhood of Frome for some time'. When Sergeant Smith searched William Maggs' house he discovered a large quantity of sugar, soap and cheese, all apparently stolen.

Despite protesting their innocence, and with only flimsy circumstantial evidence, the Magistrates sent the trio for trial at the Somerset Spring Assizes in Wells, charged with the murder of Sarah Watts.

The trial was held before Mr Justice Erle over two days in April 1852, but the evidence continued to be circumstantial; the handkerchief could not be traced with certainty to any of the prisoners, and each had a good alibi for the day on which the murder had been committed. Maggs, Sparrow and Hurd were found not guilty and left the court still protesting their innocence.

## AN AUTUMN STORM
*The calm waters off Burnham at the mouth of the River Parrett, shown here a century ago, rapidly turned into a raging sea on the night of 1–2 October 1895.*

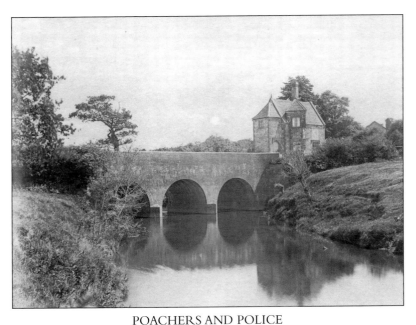

## POACHERS AND POLICE
*The alleged poachers drove their horse and trap furiously over Yeovil Bridge to avoid arrest in the early hours of 15 July 1893.*

THE FORGER OF MARK

*A photograph of the village of Mark, (c. 1900), in which Robert Fry's counterfeiting operation was brought to an abrupt end in June 1818.*

### THREE SHOCKING MURDERS
*William Bridle, the governor of Ilchester Gaol, when James Marsh was
hanged on 8 April 1816 for the savage murder of Robert Parsons.*
<small>Illustration from Hunt's Investigation at Ilchester Gaol (1821)</small>

## GORE LANGTON'S OLD TROUSERS,
## AND OTHER SURPRISING STORIES
*Police Sergeant Powell testified that he saw the butcher driving
furiously along Station Road in Ilminster late on 26 September 1900.*

## THE WIDCOMBE BRIDGE DISASTER
*Crowds lined the banks of the River Avon to view the wreckage of the
Widcombe Bridge following its catastrophic collapse on 6 June 1877.*

## THE STONING OF A SCHOOLMASTER

*It was alleged that Mr Robert Higham, the Headmaster of Reckleford School in Yeovil (seen here with his staff in 1880), had encouraged boys from the school to stone Mr Charles Hemmings, one of the assistant teachers.*

## A SUPPOSED CASE OF POISONING

*On a dark November night in 1851, the corpse of Samuel Rice was exhumed from Chard churchyard following rumours of his death from poisoning.*

S J. Speller    PAUL St & CATHERINE HILL

THE NOTORIOUS MAGGS AND SPARROW
*In the 1850s, William Maggs and William Sparrow formed a gang which
'infested' the town of Frome, shown here in a drawing from 1888.*

## THE TRIAL OF MRS JANE LEIGH PERROT

*Jane Austen's aunt, Mrs Jane Leigh Perrot, was charged with stealing a card of white lace from a shop in the city of Bath, seen here from Beechen Cliff in the early-nineteenth century.*

## ARSON AT DUNSTER

*This photograph of Dunster at the end of the nineteenth century shows a village little changed since the case of arson in 1818.*

## HE DYED IN THE KING'S SERVICE

*Memorials in Poyntington church to Sir Thomas Malet and his
son Baldwin who 'dyed in the King's Service' in 1645.*

## THE CASE OF THE STOLEN TOOTH EXTRACTORS

*The Borough, Yeovil, (c. 1914), where the tooth extractors
were stolen from Fitzherbert Rudolphus Bostick.*

## THE SURPRISING ADVENTURES OF A MONMOUTH REBEL
*An old photograph of the site of the Battle of Sedgemoor where the
Duke of Monmouth's rebel army was defeated in July 1685.*

## JAMES MARTIN AND THE FLOOD OF '94
*The wreckage of James Martin's delivery cart, with the dead horse still in harness.*

DEATHS ON THE LINE

*As his locomotive approached Marston Magna Station, Driver Edward Johnson saw a dark shape on the line ahead, and shutting off steam put the engine in reverse. The station closed in the 1960s.*

THE FIGHT AT PYE CORNER

*Under a hail of stones and blows from heavy sticks, the West Coker men were driven along the lane from the Pye Corner Inn.*

MARIA BAGNALL,

Who fell by the Hand of an Assassin at Bath
a Martyr to her Integrity Janry 26 1828.

Publish'd as the Act directs, by L Gahagan Bath March 29, 1828.

## A HORRID MURDER IN BATH

*Mr Gahagan, sculptor, made a detailed drawing of the corpse of
Maria Bagnall on the morning of her murder in January 1828.*

Brympton House & Lake.

WEYMOUTH

## IF ONLY THEY HAD BEEN ABLE TO SWIM
*Eleanor Ponsonby drowned in the tranquil lake at Brympton House, whereas Thomas Old died in the sea near the crowds on Weymouth beach.*

## THE FATAL FIGHT AT THE QUEEN'S HEAD

*Following the fight in the Queen's Head on a November evening in 1843, a badly beaten George Hallett was last seen walking through Milborne Port towards Sherborne.*

UP BEFORE THE BENCH
*On 10 February 1857 Anthony Wills assaulted Henry Sweet at the Club Room
of the Bell Inn in the village of Merriott shown here about a hundred years ago.*

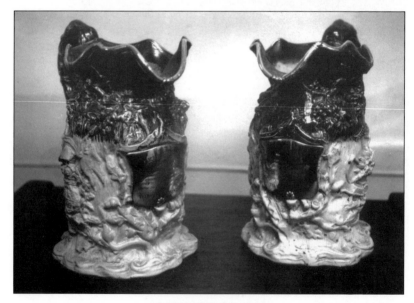

THE RIOT OF 1831
*Two of the jugs presented to each member of the Mudford Troop of Yeomanry
by Yeovil townspeople for their action in putting down the riot.*

## THE SHOCKING DEATH OF SERGEANT DENTY
*The old rifle range where Sergeant Denty was fatally injured in October 1862.*

## TEN AIR RAIDS
*The funeral of Patrol Officer Charles Gillard who was killed
in the sixth air raid on Yeovil on Good Friday 1941.*

ALL WHO GO DOWN TO THE SEA IN SHIPS
*Young Midshipman John Jacobs from Somerton (seen here in 1812) was lost in a violent storm on Christmas Day 1811.*

The killer of fourteen-year-old Sarah Watts would never be brought to justice but the 'notorious' Maggs and Sparrow would soon be back in the news.

Just over two months later in the early hours of Sunday 13 June, James White was guarding his potato patch in the garden at the back of Stony Street, in Frome, because during the night before some of his precious crop had been stolen. Suddenly he saw two shadowy figures creep across the garden and disappear over the high wall into Thomas Bunn's premises. James White roused three of his neighbours, and hiding behind some bushes, they awaited the return of the intruders. They had not long to wait, and as the two shadows slipped back over the wall the four watchers ran to seize them. In the violent struggle which followed, the two intruders were recognised as William Maggs and William Sparrow, but both managed to escape, and disappeared into the night leaving behind a large cheese wrapped in a sack. In the light of the following morning, the cheese was tracked to Mr Plaister's grocer's cheese store, and the search was on for the two burglars.

On Monday morning, Edward Newport, the Frome constable, and a number of assistants, set out to search Maggs' house, and on effecting an entry were confronted by Mrs Maggs, described as 'a complete virago', armed with a loaded gun swearing to shoot the constable. Edward Newport was no coward, and leaping forward wrestled the gun from the 'virago', and then proceeded to search the house. Loose floorboards in the bedroom were taken up and revealed a large number of items, including twine, cotton, sandpaper and about 300 keys and pick locks of all descriptions. Meanwhile search parties were combing the countryside for the two fugitives, and on Thursday Sparrow was captured in Bedcombe Wood near Longleat, and taken to Shepton Mallet Gaol. There were reports of Maggs being seen in the same area, but he would remain at large for only a few more days.

On 25 October 1852, William Maggs was brought before the Michaelmas Quarter Sessions, charged with two counts of stealing milk from cows belonging to James Allard and Miss Hoddinott. In both cases, the farmers believed that their cows had been milked during several nights, and a watch was kept to find the culprits. The night of 4 June was bright moonlight, and watchman Charles Weaver could identify the two figures who had crept into the field and began to milk one of the cows – they were William Maggs and William Sparrow. An alibi by Zacharia Starr, that Maggs was with him that night in the Red Lion Inn at Trowbridge, was dismissed after the Sergeant of the Trowbridge police, swore that there was no hostelry called the Red Lion in the town.

William Maggs was found guilty on both counts. For the first he received one month's imprisonment with hard labour, and for the second he was sentenced to fifteen years' transportation to Australia. The court was told that Maggs would also be tried at the Somerset Spring Assizes for the burglary at Mr Plaister's cheese store on 13 June last.

William Sparrow was similarly tried at the Quarter Sessions for the theft of the milk, and received the same sentences as his notorious companion in crime; he was also down for trial at the Spring Assizes for the burglary.

Early in the morning of Monday 21 March 1853, William Maggs, accompanied by sixteen-year-old John Wilson who was awaiting transportation to Australia for ten years, broke out of the County Gaol at Wilton, Taunton. The two convicts occupied adjoining cells in the upper corridor of the gaol, and during the weeks of their imprisonment, they had made a hole in the 4½ inch brick work of the roofs of their cells using tools made from forks and spoons. The two men got out onto the roof of the gaol, crept along to the back of the clock tower, and clambered 30 feet down a drainpipe to the airing yard. Crossing the yard, they climbed up the outside of the tread-mill using the iron window bars as footholds, clambered over the 18-inch projecting eaves some 40 feet from the ground, and with a rope made from the strands of oakum they picked in the work shed, let themselves down over the wall of the gaol.

The escape was discovered at six o'clock in the morning and immediately bills, with the description of the two fugitives and offering a £20 reward for their capture, were circulated throughout the district. Liberty was short and not very sweet. At about half past four the same afternoon, two men by name of Brown and Jarvis found the two convicts in a field at Fitzroy, about 4 miles from Taunton. William Maggs and his companion could not have picked a worse day to break out, because it was unseasonably very cold and snowing. The two convicts were only wearing their shirts, as all other garments were removed at night, and carrying a small piece of bread for sustenance, Maggs and Wilson were taken without a struggle, as wet, cold and exhausted, they left the ditch in which they had been hiding, and made for a small barn. At nine o'clock on the Monday evening, the pair were brought back to the County Gaol tied to a cart. A fortnight later, Willam Maggs appeared at the Somerset Spring Assizes in Taunton charged with the burglary at Mr Plaister's cheese store, found guilty and was sentenced to be transported to Australia for life. This time there would be no escape.

Four months later, in August 1853, William Sparrow appeared at the Somerset Summer Assizes in Wells, charge with the burglary at Mr Plaister's cheese store. He was described by the *Taunton Courier* as 'A cunning, hardened villain. His hair had been closely cropped, and he looked an undoubted "jail bird"'. Sparrow was found guilty, and although he 'whined for mercy', the Judge responded by saying, 'Oh, you're a very desperate character. I must inflict a sentence on you that will rid the country of you for a very long time. The sentence upon you is that you will be transported for ten years to take effect on the expiration of the former sentence of fifteen years!' The *Taunton Courier* commented, 'The country is, therefore, rid of the pest for twenty-five years.'

However, the country had not quite rid itself of 'the pest'. Early on the Tuesday morning following his sentence, William Sparrow broke out of the small and inadequate gaol adjoining the Wells Town Hall, and made off in the company of a fellow convict called Bird. On discovering the escape, bills with their description and offering a £20 reward for the convicts' recapture, were circulated immediately throughout the area. Between two and three o'clock that afternoon, Henry Stevens of Cook Mill Farm, Pilton, was returning home on horseback when, at the bottom of Lambridge Hill, on the Glastonbury to Shepton Mallet road, the farmer passed two men walking towards Shepton Mallet. Having read the wanted bills, he was certain that one of the men was William Sparrow and, turning his horse. caught up with the pair and chatted to them about the weather and crops. Reaching the four crossroads leading to Pilton, Sparrow made an excuse to go into a field, and climbed over the gate. Leaving Bird in the road, Farmer Stevens rode on towards Shepton Mallet hoping to find enough assistance to return and capture the two convicts. At last the farmer obtained several helpers, and they tracked the villains up the Compton road towards Cannard's Grave, and into a field of wheat. Following their footmarks, Sparrow and Bird were found hiding in the standing wheat near the top of the field. Despite some scuffling with Sparrow, the two men were taken into custody and lodged in Shepton Mallet Gaol. William Sparrow was at last on his way to Australia.

# THE TRIAL OF MRS JANE LEIGH PERROT

Despite the chill of the late March morning, the fashionably dressed women walking sedately through Regency Taunton could have been making their way to an early assembly to partake of tea and engage in polite conversation. However, the slim, middle-aged Mrs Jane Leigh Perrot, an aunt of the novelist Jane Austen, who walked with her elegant companions from their lodgings at the London Inn to the Assize Hall, had an appointment with a Judge and jury. Before this day was out, Mrs Leigh Perrot would either return with her companions to the comfort of the London Inn or be in Ilchester Gaol, possibly awaiting the hangman's rope or the long deadly voyage to a penal colony in Australia.

At eight o'clock on the morning of Saturday, 29 March 1800, Mrs Jane Leigh Perrot, now accompanied by her wealthy husband and several of her lady companions, entered the 'prisoner's pen' in the Assize Hall and before the Judge, Mr Justice Lawrence, the jury, and several hundred spectators crammed into every available space, pleaded not guilty to the indictment of stealing a card of white lace, valued at 20 shillings, from the shop of Miss Elizabeth Gregory in Bath Street in the city of Bath.

On trial for her life, for it was a hanging offence to steal goods valued at more than five shillings from a shop, Mrs Leigh Perrot was allowed to be seated and Mr Gibbs, counsel for the Crown, called the first prosecution witness Miss Elizabeth Gregory. She stated that she owned a haberdasher and milliner's shop in Bath Street and a plan was presented showing the layout of the premises (see page 69).

The witness stated that between one and two o'clock on 8 August 1799, Mrs Leigh Perrot had come into the shop and asked to look at some black lace she had seen the day before. The lace was produced and a sale was agreed at £1.19s.. Miss Gregory explained that at that time she had been standing behind the left- hand counter in the position shown G on the plan and Mrs Leigh Perrot opposite at place B. The witness stated that she had then called her shopman, Charles Filby, to come and measure and wrap up the purchase. Miss Gregory had then returned to her counting desk at place D. Shortly after, Charles Filby came for change for the five pound note tendered by Mrs Leigh Perrot for the lace, and then she had gone downstairs to the kitchen for dinner. About ten minutes later the shopman came down and told her that Mrs Leigh Perrot had taken a card of white lace and left without paying for

# PLAN of Mifs GREGORY's SHOP.
### (Late WILLIAM SMITH's.)

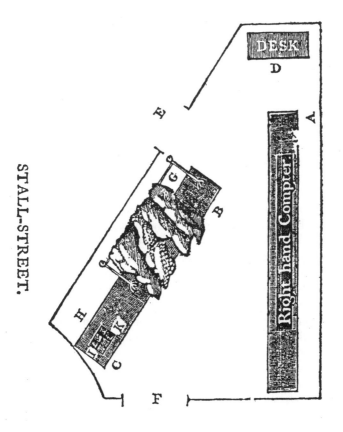

STALL-STREET.

DESK
D

E

A

Right hand Compter

G

B

H

K

C

DESK

F

BATH-STREET.

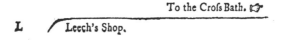

To the Crofs Bath.

L    Leech's Shop.

it. Miss Gregory testified that about a quarter of an hour later she saw the prisoner and her husband walk past the shop. The witness described how she had rushed out and, catching up with the couple, demanded to know whether Mrs Leigh Perrot had a card of white lace as well as the black. Mrs Leigh Perrot had hotly denied this, but when she produced the parcel from under her cloak, Miss Gregory saw the end of a piece of white lace protruding from the open end of what appeared to have been a hastily wrapped package. Mrs Leigh Perrot, who appeared shocked and flustered, denied taking the lace and suggested that the shopman must have included the white piece by mistake. Removing the white lace from the parcel, the witness saw the private shop mark on the article and, after accusing Mrs Leigh Perrot of stealing the piece, took it back to the shop; she then went to the Town Hall to lay an information for theft. However, because the Magistrates had been fully occupied with the problems being caused by the ill-disciplined soldiers of several regiments passing through Bath, Miss Gregory stated that she had been prevented from laying the information for six days despite going to the Town Hall every day.

The next witness was the shopman, Charles Filby, who said that he had worked for Miss Gregory for six months. On the day concerned he had been sitting at the left-hand counter, place H, measuring cards of black and white lace, putting the private shop mark on each one, and packing them in boxes I and K on the counter. He had been called to the top end of the shop, to serve Mrs Leigh Perrot and measure the piece of black lace she had bought. The witness described how he had rolled the lace on a piece of card, wrapped it in paper, folded and secured each end of the parcel. Charles Filby stated that he handed the parcel to the prisoner who gave him a five pound note, which he took to Miss Gregory at the counting desk. Whilst he waited for the change his back had been to Mrs Leigh Perrot, but on turning around the witness noticed that she was now standing at the end of the left-hand counter, place C, and in front of the box of lace. Charles Filby stated that when he returned with the change he had walked behind the rack of handkerchiefs and shawls standing on the left counter, and for a moment Mrs Leigh Perrot was out of his sight. The witness testified that to his surprise he saw Mrs Leigh Perrot quickly snatch one of the cards of white lace from the box with her left hand and hide it under her short cloak. Charles Filby stated that he had placed the change on the counter but Mrs Leigh Perrot had kept her left hand hidden under the cloak even though this meant both holding the parcel of black lace and picking up the small coins with her right hand. She had then left the shop. After telling Miss Gregory what he had seen, the witness had remained in the kitchen for some time but when he returned to the shop he saw Miss Gregory holding the card of white lace. Charles Filby stated that he had been sent to look for Mrs Leigh Perrot and shortly after he saw her with her husband turning the corner of the Abbey churchyard. The couple then parted but when Mrs Leigh Perrot saw him she had run back to her husband who, when asked his name, had told Charles Filby that he lived at 1 Paragon Buildings and his name was on the door.

Having completed his evidence Charles Filby came under intensive cross-examination by the defence counsel who did their best to discredit him. He agreed that he had failed in business and had been twice bankrupted but he had satisfied most of his creditors. The witness also agreed that on one occasion he had sold a veil to a Miss Blagrove and she had brought one back the following day saying that she had found two in the parcel. He could recall no other occasion when he had put up more articles than were purchased. Charles Filby strongly denied a suggestion by the defence counsel that he not wrapped the black lace in front of Mrs Leigh Perrot but had gone back down to the end of the left-hand counter and done this by the box of lace.

The prosecution's third and final witness was eighteen-year-old Sarah Raines, the shop apprentice, who said that she had been working at the same counter as Filby and saw him wrap the piece of black lace and hand the parcel to the prisoner. At this point the Judge interrupted and asked the witness whether she was certain that only the black lace had been place in the parcel to which she firmly replied, 'Yes my Lord I am!'

In 1800, a defence counsel could only examine and cross-examine the Crown's witnesses and call witnesses for the defence; he could not present the defence, which had to be put by the defendant. The Judge now addressed Mrs Leigh Perrot and told her that if she had anything to say in her defence now was the time. Mrs Leigh Perrot was in a state of collapse and her voice was so faint and hesitant that her counsel was asked to repeat what she said. She told the court that she had fortune enough to:

gratify all my wishes. Blessed in the affection of the most generous man as a husband, what could induce me to commit such a crime? Depraved indeed must  the mind be, that under such circumstances, could be so culpable. You will hear from my noble and truly respectable friends what has been my conduct and character for a long series of years. You will hear what has been, and what is now their opinion of me. Can you suppose that disposition so totally altered as to lose all recollection of the situation I held in society, to hazard for this meanness, character and reputation, or to endanger the health and peace of mind of a husband whom I would die for? You have heard their evidence against me, I shall make no comments upon it. I shall leave the talk where I am certain it will be executed with justice and mercy. I know my own oath, in this case, is inadmissible, but I call upon God whom you all adore, to attest that I am innocent of this charge, and may he reward or punish me as I speak true or false, in denying it! I call that God to witness, that I did not know that I had the lace in my possession, nor did I know it when Miss Gregory accosted me in the Street. I have nothing more to add.

Mrs Leigh Perrot's counsel now called Miss Blagrave who recalled that on 19 September 1799, at about five o'clock in the evening, she had bought a veil in Miss Gregory's shop and had been served by a tall shopman whom she now knew to be Charles Filby. When she opened the parcel she found two veils instead of one and took the second back the next day. She did not know Mrs Leigh Perrot and had never spoken to her.

Next came the character witnesses who included George Vansittart Esq., MP for Berkshire, where the Leigh Perrot's had an estate, Lord Braybrook, Mr Annesley MP for Reading, several clergymen, doctors and ladies, all of whom testified that they were closely acquainted with Mrs Leigh Perrot and spoke in the highest terms of her fine character.

The Judge then began his summing up. He stated that he considered the case had been fully proved if the jury believed the testimony of the Crown's witnesses. There was some doubt about the good character of the witness, Filby, but his evidence had not been contradicted by the defence. Filby's evidence had also been corroborated by Miss Gregory and Sarah Raines. The Judge then referred to the very high character given to the prisoner by her witnesses, but if the jury were satisfied with the Crown's evidence and believed the witnesses, they were bound to find the prisoner guilty. However, the Judge went on to observe that the prisoner, by returning and passing by Miss Gregory's shop still carrying the parcel when she could have gone home and hidden the lace, did not seem to be the conduct of a guilty person. The fact that the prisoner appeared shocked and flustered when accused of stealing the lace should not be taken as an indication of guilt, because anyone suddenly stopped and so accused in the street could act in a similar manner. He also drew attention to the evidence of Miss Blagrave that Filby had once by mistake put up two veils in a parcel. In conclusion, the Judge advised the jury that if they had any reason to disbelieve the Crown's witnesses or had any doubt of the prisoner's guilt, they should take into account the very excellent character given to her and which should weigh in favour of an acquittal.

The Jury deliberated for about a quarter of an hour and found Mrs Jane

Leigh Perrot not guilty. She would be returning to the comfort of the London Inn and then home to 1 Paragon Buildings.

Mrs Leigh Perrot had spent seven months in Ilchester Gaol awaiting trial but her incarceration was not so unpleasant as might be imagined. Her husband had been with her for the whole time and, being an extremely wealthy man, the prison accommodation was made as comfortable as possible.

Before and after the trial there were allegations that the Leigh Perrots had been the victims of a failed extortion plan and that perjured evidence was given. However the allegations were not raised by the defence counsel and were never tested in court.

At the Spring Assizes of 1800 the following capital sentences were passed:

John Rugg, for stealing a brown mare – Death

Robert Burnet, for stealing half a bushel of wheat – Death

Jeremiah Phillips, for sheep stealing – Death

Thomas Coles and John Trebly, for housebreaking and stealing property to the value of £90 – Death

John Chamberlain, for stealing cloth from bleaching grounds – Death

William Smoaker, for stealing banknotes – Death

James Stock, for housebreaking – Death

William Walling, for assaulting and robbing Sarah Snelgrove – Death

William Phillips, for stealing three sheep – Death

Mary Fennell, for robbing Mr Herbert of two guineas – Death

The death sentences were carried out on Coles, Trebly and Walling; the others were reprieved and transported to Australia.

# ARSON AT DUNSTER

On 12 August 1818, fourteen-year-old Betty Nicholls went on trial before Mr Justice Park at the Somerset Assizes in Wells, charged with three counts of setting fire to property, including a linhay, owned by Thomas Thorn at Dunster. If found guilty, Betty would hang, or at best be transported to Australia for life, or a very long time if the Judge was merciful; arson was a capital offence. Standing in the dock with the girl was a young man called Martin Wynne, charged as an accessory before the fact in abetting Betty Nicholls in committing the crimes. Both pleaded not guilty. By way of explanation, a linhay, was a double-storeyed open sided building comprising a cattle or cart shed on the ground floor, with a hayloft above, most commonly found in South West England.

Prosecuting counsel, Mr Adams, read the first indictment, and his colleague, Mr Serjeant Pell outlined the case. He stated that on 7 January 1818, the house called the Little Linhay, and owned by a farmer, Mr Thomas Thorn, caught fire. The prisoner, Betty Nicholls, had been a servant of the farmer and had lived in his household for some five or six years. Martin Wynne, had also lived with the family as a farm servant for nearly a year, but had left service about two years before. He had then occupied a cottage owned by Thomas Thorn, but the farmer had now turned him out.

On Sunday 11 January last, Thomas Thorn and his family had left for church at about a quarter to eleven o'clock, leaving Betty Nichols, servant Martha Wedlake, and the farmer's mother-in-law in the farmhouse. Mr Serjeant Pell stated that Thomas Thorn had been called from church and told that there was a fire at the farm. On arriving home he had found the Pond Court linhay next to his house and its contents of hay ablaze and a total loss; the farmhouse was also damaged. During the subsequent enquiries, Betty Nicholls said that she had seen a man, whom she did not know, come out of the Pond Court and go away down the Long Meadow.

Serjeant Pell called his first witness, the servant Martha Wedlake, who recalled Mr Thorn and his family going to church. Before her master had left for church, Martin Wynne had come to the house, and stayed with Betty Nicholls in the back kitchen. Some time after eleven o'clock, Betty Nicholls had gone out to kill a turkey for the Sunday meal, and which she brought back some five or six minutes later. The girl had plucked the turkey, and then put it on the dresser, asking the witness to finish preparing the bird as she had found one of the pigs was missing and was going to look for it. Martha Wedlake stated that Betty Nicholls had gone out the front door, leaving it open, and the witness had stayed in the kitchen reading. She could not recall where Martin Wynne had gone. About a quarter of an hour later, the servant stated that she had seen smoke and going out into the yard, saw Betty Nicholls looking at the hay burning in the Pond Court linhay.

The next witness, Eliza Thorn, the farmer's wife, recollected that Wynne had come to the house early on the Sunday morning to settle up what he owed on quitting her husband's service. He had left, but then came back at about 10 o'clock, to rectify a mistake. Eliza Thorn also stated that none of the pigs was missing, because she had notice they were all in the higher orchard when the family had left for church.

Jane Thorn, the eight-year-old farmer's daughter, followed her mother into the witness box. Despite her tender years, the court was satisfied of 'her competence to receive an oath'. The child stated that she remembered the Sunday when the linhay was on fire. She told how she had been standing in the passage outside the back kitchen, the door of which was partly open, and saw Wynne drinking a pint of cider with Betty Nicholls. Little Jane remembered him saying to Betty Nicholls. 'Mind and do what I told you to do.'

A boy called Thomas Phillips, of Lower Marsh, now took the stand. He stated that at about ten o'clock on the Sunday morning, he had walked a little way with Martin Wynne, and had mentioned two recent fires at Mr Thorn's farm. The prisoner Wynne had replied that the linhay 'would be on fire the next'.

Witness, Thomas Lovell, recalled working with Martin Wynne on 4 January, and talking about Mr Thorn. Wynne had told how the farmer had accused him of stealing his turnips, and stated angrily that 'He would be damned if he would be a match for Thomas Thorn before it was long.'

Dunster innkeeper, John Strong, recollected Martin Wynne coming into his house on the day of the fire. When he said that he wondered what rascal it was who had set Mr Thorn's house on fire, the prisoner had replied that he did not know, but 'Thank God, he was hedging with Thomas Dunn – for as Mr Thorn and he had angry words, he might have thought something of him.'

Another witness, George Green, said that he had seen Wynne on the Monday afternoon, and they had talked about the fire. The prisoner had commented that  he had been looking all day for them to come and apprehend him.

The Constable of the Hundred, William Little, testified that at about seven o'clock on the Monday evening, he had gone into the George Inn and Martin Wynne was one of the customers. The constable recalled that when the prisoner saw him he began to shake and denied that he had anything to do with the fire. William Little stated that he had said nothing about the fire, and in fact he had not suspected Wynne.

Witness, William Hole recalled seeing Martin Wynne in the courtyard of the farm after the fire had broken out.

The last witness, Ann Pope, another servant of Thomas Thorn, remembered Betty Nichols saying on the Sunday morning, just before the family went to church, 'Suppose the house should catch fire – it would be fun to see the people tumbling out of church one over the other.' Ann Pope had exclaimed in reply, 'God forbid it should happen. One would think you had a fire in it!'

When the last witness left the stand, prosecuting counsel, Mr Adams, stated that he had offered all the evidence he had to establish the charge. However, he was anxious to have the Judge's opinion on whether Betty Nicholls' confession could be presented. This had been obtained after she had been examined by the Magistrates, and after Thomas Thorn had threatened to tie her to the leg of the table if she did not confess the truth about the fire. Mr Justice Park, replied that the confession could not be received in evidence, because it had been made under duress after Betty Nicholls had denied the charges under oath before the Magistrates. Following the Judge's summing up, the jury found Betty Nichols and Martin Wynne Not Guilty.

However, there were two more charges of arson against Betty Nicholls, to which she pleaded not guilty, and the court proceeded to deal with the first indictment. The prosecution submitted that on 9 January 1818, Betty Nicholls was seen by three witnesses, going towards the hayloft of Thomas Thorn's upper linhay, with her hands under her apron, and when she came back her hands were no longer concealed, and the hay was on fire. An old tin pot which was usually hung up outside the farmhouse was found near the spot where the fire had started. It was alleged that she had carried some burning material in the pot to start the fire.

The jury, however, acquitted Betty Nicholls, as they believed she had no malice towards her master, Thomas Thorn.

The second charge accused Betty Nicholls of setting fire to Thomas Thorn's premises two days before on 7 January 1818, but when the prosecution declined to call any evidence in support of the indictment, the case was dismissed.

Mr Justice Park now turned his stern attention to the small fourteen-year-old servant standing below him in the dock. The Judge stated that now he was no longer prevented by law, he would say that without doubt Betty Nicholls was guilty of having committed the three serious offences. Her own confession, which could not in point of law be used against her, proved hers was the hand that committed the wicked deeds. Mr Justice Park then turned his full attention to Martin Wynne, and observed that there was every reason to believe that he had from 'some malice, or other, been an abetter in these shocking transactions'.

Betty Nicholls was taken weeping from the dock, and two very lucky young people disappeared into the mists of time.

# HE DYED IN THE KING'S SERVICE

Poyntington was part of the County of Somerset until 31 March 1896 when it was transferred to Dorset and, but for the provisions of the Local Government Act 1888, would today be part of South Somerset. I have therefore taken the liberty to include this tale as the events which follow occurred when the village and its people were Somerset folk.

The church of All Saints and the village of Poyntington lie quietly in a secluded valley sheltered by steep hillsides, but in 1645 this rural peace was shattered as one of two painted plaques on the wall of the south aisle of the church testifies. One of the plaques commemorates the Lord of the Manor, Sir Thomas Malet, and the other remembers his son Baldwin.

Sir Thomas Malet was a Judge prominent in the service of King Charles I, and following the defeat of the Royalist cause in the Great Civil War, he was imprisoned in the Tower of London until the Restoration of Charles II in 1660, when he was released There is a story that during the Civil War his wife, Lady Malet, suffered the indignity of having her wedding ring taken by a Parliamentary trooper and, in protest, she wore a ring made from horn until her death.

The memorial to Baldwin Malet bears a coat of arms and the following words:

Baldwin Malet, second sonne of Sr Thomas Malet
dyed in the King's Service the 3 day of June
An: Dni. 1646 in the twentieth yeare of his age

There is a little mystery about Baldwin's memorial. The Parish Register, much decayed but still decipherable, in the Dorset Record Office in Dorchester, shows the date of the burial of Baldwin Malet was on 3 June 1645 and not 1646, as shown on the memorial. The explanation is probably a mistake by the craftsman or sponsors when both memorials were made following the death of Sir Thomas in 1665. It is unlikely that Baldwin's memorial would have been made and displayed during the Commonwealth of his father's enemy, Oliver Cromwell.

By June 1645, the Civil War had reached a crucial stage, and although most of the West Country was in Royalist hands, a number of Parliamentary garrisons still held out, including Taunton which was withstanding a savage siege conducted by Lord George Goring. In April, Parliament's recently formed New Model Army commanded by Sir Thomas Fairfax, advanced west to relieve Taunton, and by early May was in Blandford poised to advance north. However on 7 May, Fairfax was ordered to join Oliver Cromwell to engage the main Royalist army which had left its Oxford stronghold, and had begun to campaign in the Midlands. Six regiments were left in Dorset and by early June they were occupying the Chard area waiting to raise the siege of Taunton.

At this time Sherborne Castle, some 3 miles south of Poyntington, was a Royalist stronghold and a major influence on the district, including the local 'Club Men'. The 'Clubs' were springing up in many parts of the country, now weary of three years of war and its attendant destruction, and were formed by local people seeking to protect their towns and villages against the depredations of both sides of the conflict. In Somerset the majority of 'Club Men' were anti-Royalist, following the activities of Lord George Goring's army, but in Dorset and along the Somerset border in the Sherborne area, they were strongly influenced by the local Royalist gentry and churchmen. The Dorset 'Clubs' were prominent in attacking Parliamentary troops and their lines of communication throughout the county.

The story of Baldwin Malet recounts that on 2 June 1645, a body of Parliamentary infantry was moving north through the area in the direction of Wincanton, possibly en route to join Fairfax and Cromwell, when the Royalist villagers of Poyntington attacked. Baldwin is reported to have arrived at the scene of the fight, fully armoured, and leaping his horse over a gate, charged into the middle of the Parliamentary soldiers. After killing some 20 of his enemies, he was hacked down and slain; Baldwin's corpse was returned to the Manor house just an hour after he had left it, and was buried the following day for fear of plague breaking out in the summer heat. The scene of the fight, adjoining the road to neighbouring Oborn, is reputed to be haunted by headless soldiers and a headless woman — a camp follower perhaps?

# THE CASE OF THE STOLEN
# TOOTH EXTRACTORS

In February 1916, a rather strange case appeared in the Yeovil Magistrates Court. Before the Bench was a sergeant of the Queen's Own Dorset Yeomanry stationed in Sherborne, charged with stealing at Yeovil on Saturday 19 February 1916, a pair of dentist's molar forceps, the property of Fitzherbert Rudolphus Bostick, described as a 'travelling tooth extractor'.

Donald Martin, a clerk employed by Messrs Aplin and Barrett, was the first witness, and testified that on the Saturday evening in question, he saw Mr Bostick with an open stand in the borough, at which he was extracting teeth and selling tooth powder. There was a chair at the back of the stand upon which were laid out about a dozen pairs of forceps. The witness observed the accused in the crowd, and saw him walk up to the chair, pick up a pair of forceps, put them in his pocket and walk away down Silver Street. Donald Martin went on to say that the sergeant had taken the forceps quite openly and anyone could have seen him do so.

Fitzherbert Adolphus Bostick told the court that he was extracting teeth and selling tooth powder from his stand. He had placed his pairs of forceps on the chair behind him and therefore could not see anyone picking them up. He had not seen the sergeant take the instrument but someone in the crowd had shouted out that a soldier had picked up a pair of his forceps and gone down Silver Street. Mr Bostick stated that he had run after the soldier, whom he identified as the sergeant, and on stopping him asked for the return of the forceps. The sergeant quite openly took them out of his pocket and handed them back saying that they had been given to him by a man.

At this point, Superintendent House, told the Bench that he had just received a message from the officer commanding the Queen's Own Dorset Yeomanry at Sherborne, stating that the sergeant was required immediately for isolation and should not have been in Yeovil. The soldier was ordered to return to Sherborne, and the case adjourned for eight days, binding the accused over in his own recognisance of £5.

Eight days later, the case came back to the Magistrates who were told that the officer in charge of the military laboratory at the Nothe, Weymouth, had advised that the sergeant would be detailed for isolation for another ten days to a fortnight. The Bench decided to adjourn the case until 7 March. The record is silent on the reasons for the sergeant's isolation.

On 7 March, the sergeant duly appeared before the Town Magistrates, and after the evidence given at the first hearing was read, the accused elected for the case to be dealt with summarily, and pleaded not guilty.

In a sworn statement, the sergeant stated that he had been walking past Mr Redwood's shop in the borough, and had just stopped to light his pipe, when he felt something drop into his pocket. Looking around he saw a boy running away and feeling in his pocket found the pair of dental forceps. The sergeant went on to say that he placed no value on the instrument, and walked on down Silver Street thinking the whole episode was a prank. As for the statement that he was seen taking the forceps, the sergeant exclaimed that this was a lie, and he was only restrained from hitting Mr Bostick when he was accused of theft because he was a sergeant in uniform. Asked whether the accused was drunk when brought to the police station, Superintendent House replied that he seemed somewhat stupid and very stubborn.

Major R.C. Bately, the sergeant's commanding officer, told the Bench that the soldier had risen to his non-commissioned rank through constant good work, sobriety and attention to his duties, and was given an exemplary character. During the time the sergeant had been stationed in Sherborne, he had been in charge of hundreds of pounds' worth of government property, and had never been known to misappropriate any of it.

The Magistrates bound the sergeant over for six months in view of the high character he had been given by his commanding officer.

# THE SURPRISING ADVENTURES
# OF A MONMOUTH REBEL

The defeat of the Duke of Monmouth's army at the Battle of Sedgemoor in July 1685 and the Bloody Assizes of Judge Jeffreys which followed, have long remained part of the folk memory of the West Country. A number of accounts have been left of the battle and the shocking events which followed, but perhaps none finer is the remarkable story of a carpenter from Stoford, near Yeovil, by name of John Coad. He left a tale of suffering and surprising courage by an ordinary man caught up in Monmouth's Rebellion and its aftermath.

John Coad (sometimes known as Thomas) was a member of the Somerset Militia, and was called out when James, Duke of Monmouth, landed at Lyme Regis and raised his rebellion against the unpopular Roman Catholic monarch, James II. On 13 June 1685, John left his wife and children to march with the militia against the rebel force assembling at Lyme Regis. He was a strong Dissenting Protestant and, in common with hundreds of his countrymen, was much in sympathy with the cause of the Duke of Monmouth. During the long march towards Chard, John Coad made up his mind that if the opportunity arose, he would transfer his allegiance to the Protestant Duke. The bravado and foul language of his fellow militiamen strengthened the desire of this deeply religious man to enter the Duke's service.

On reaching Chard, the militia went into camp and the carpenter decided, after wrestling with his conscience all night and earnestly praying for direction and guidance, to join the rebel cause as soon as he could. This was treason, and to desert would mean leaving his wife, children and property back in Stoford to fate. John Coad must have spent a very difficult time trying to decide on the best course of action, but at last he made up his mind to join the rebels.

The following day, the militia advanced from Chard towards Axminster where the rebel army was gathering, and by now was a fairly formidable force. The militia did not prove to be the lions of a few days before, and when the rebel army advanced towards their positions, the militiamen decided that discretion was the better part of valour, and withdrew with some speed. It was in this confusion that John Coad saw his chance, and at a suitable moment he slipped away and joined Monmouth's rebels. As a man with some military training and with weapons, he was welcomed as a useful addition to the

Duke's cause, and with the retreat of the militia, there were high hopes of an early victory.

John Coad was enlisted in Monmouth's Red Regiment, and marched with the rebel army to Taunton, then on to Bridgwater, and saw his first action in a skirmish with the royal army at Keynsham. The royal troops were now appearing in some strength in Somerset, and the rebels fell back to Norton St Philip where John was to see action once again, and the start of his many trials and tribulations.

In the hotly contested action at Norton St Philip, John Coad was shot in the left wrist and left breast. Bleeding heavily he fell and was trampled on in the confusion of the fighting. More dead than alive, he was carried from the battlefield, but as his wounds were judged to be mortal, the surgeons refused to dress them and the carpenter was left to die.

That evening, Monmouth's men moved out of Norton St Philip and retreated towards Frome, but as John Coad was found to be still alive, he was thrown onto a wagon with other wounded rebels. The shaking of the wagon opened his wounds causing them to bleed afresh, and the pain was so intense he prayed for death to relieve his suffering. John's prayers, however, went unanswered, and three days later the carpenter found himself at Shepton Mallet, still alive but with his wounds undressed. It was at Shepton Mallet that a Mr Hardy, an apothecary from Lyme Regis, cut off what was left of his bloody clothing, and probing about found the musket ball still lodged in his back and cut it out. As the rebel army was still on the move, there was no opportunity for John's wounds to be properly treated, and this did not occur until the army stopped at Middlezoy, near Bridgwater.

During the retreat from Keynsham, King James had issued a proclamation granting a pardon to any rebel who surrendered within eight days, and John Coad's wife set out to find her husband, and persuade him to seek the royal pardon. By good fortune, the couple were reunited at Middlezoy, and as the carpenter was so disabled, he decided to quit the rebel army in the hope of obtaining the pardon within the four days left. No doubt John felt that he had done his duty, and the pain and suffering experienced during the past few days was as much as anyone could or should be required to bear for any cause; there were also his family and property to consider.

In company with his wife, John Coad left Middlezoy with a view to seeking the pardon back in Stoford, but he was taken with a violent fever, and although the couple managed to reach Long Sutton within about 10 miles of home, the carpenter was too ill to go any further. No doctor or surgeon could be found to treat his wounds, and his condition was now desperate. It does not take much imagination to see John, dirty, bloodstained and ragged, together with his wife, desperately seeking shelter but being spurned by the population who were either opposed to the rebels or too frightened to have anything to do with them. The couple eventually found lodgings in Long Sutton, and although the local midwife took pity on the wounded man, she would only help after dark. She treated his wounds and the raging fever, and probably saved his life. It is possible that at this stage John Coad was being held prisoner, because in his account he refers to lying in the house of an enemy.

By now the Battle of Sedgemoor had been fought, Monmouth's army defeated and scattered, and the regulars and loyal militia were scouring the countryside for fugitives. It was not long before soldiers were told that a wounded rebel was being held in Long Sutton, and they arrived swearing they would put the carpenter out of his misery. Later John Coad recounted that when the troopers came to the house, they charged up the stairs and into the room in which his was lying. One of the soldiers, whether intending to kill him or frighten him, fired a pistol but as it had been overcharged the weapon exploded. The soldier, injured by his exploding pistol, was taken from the room, and then for some reason the troopers took no more interest in John, even though they remained in the house for the rest of the night drinking heavily.

What happened next is quite incredible, because not only was John Coad at death's door, suffering a violent fever, shot at and abused, but the next morning the soldiers made him promise that he would pay for their drunken revelry of the night before! The troopers then departed, reporting his presence to Lord Stawel, one of the prominent royalists in Somerset, who ordered John Coad to be brought before him to be dealt with. On hearing this news, John sent his wife to an uncle, asking him to seek the assistance of his former commanding officer in the Somerset Militia, Sir Edward Phelips, to intercede for him with Lord Stawel. Sir Edward responded to the plea, and arranged for John Coad to be taken to Ilchester Gaol where the keeper kept him safe from attentions of the regulars and militia who were still ranging the area. Sir Edward Phelips must have been a merciful man, even to a deserter and a traitor, because he ordered a surgeon to take care of John Coad and, if possible, to save his life, even though he was obviously going to stand trial and face a death sentence; the carpenter had not been in time to obtain the royal pardon.

After a stay in Ilchester Gaol of some ten to eleven weeks, and although still weak and with open wounds, John Coad was taken to the Assize at Wells to face the dreaded Judge Jeffreys. Here he was imprisoned in the cathedral cloisters and expected nothing but death as a deserter and traitor who had left his colours for the rebel Duke. With some 600 other rebels, John was brought before Judge Jeffreys and condemned to death. By now the carpenter had lost all hope, and was preparing himself for the terrible fate which awaited him at the hands of the public executioner.

A few days later, however, whilst 'contemplating my future fate and praying for strength', John Coad received a visit from his sister who told him that an officer in the cathedral cloisters was calling out the names of 200 men to be transported to Jamaica, and she pressed and entreated her brother to try to get into the group. John's sister had heard only that morning, that following his execution, his body would be hung before his door at Stoford, and what an awful retribution and humiliation this would be. John Coad and his sister approached the officer who refused a bribe to put him on the list, but the man was obviously sympathetic with the carpenter's condition, and he told them that if any prisoner did not answer his name when called, John could answer and step in. Unfortunately, all the names had been called, and there appeared to be no hope of escaping the shocking fate which awaited. Providence one again intervened, because as John was taking leave of his sister, a woman from Chard told him that one of the men waiting to be transported was unwilling to go and so they changed places, with the carpenter answering to the name of the man – Jo Haker.

Thus John Coad was saved again, for the time being, and a few days later we find him in Sherborne on his way to Weymouth for transportation. Once again, however, he comes in possible harm's way because the carpenter was well known in the area, and in particular to the local constable who had no sympathy for Dissenting Protestants or rebels. The constable seeing John amongst the prisoners asked the officer in charge whether his name was on the list because, in the constable's opinion, he ought not to be there. Having seen the list and no John Coad upon it, the constable departed, but for some reason which we will never know, did not return, even though the prisoners remained in Sherborne for two days. John Coad must have spent two harrowing days and nights in the town waiting for the authorities to take him back to Wells and death, but this was not to be, and the prisoners were marched to Weymouth where they were taken on board a ship bound for Jamaica. The date was 17 October 1685, four months after the Stoford carpenter had left his hearth and home to embark upon what he had hoped would be a glorious Protestant revolution.

By now John Coad was almost certainly convinced that he stood a very good chance of escaping from England and the fate which awaited him at Wells because, once in Jamaica, it was unlikely he would be brought back many thousands of miles for execution; for many, transportation was as good as being sent to the hangman. However, before the ship sailed, some Sheriff's officers came on board and arrested one of the prisoners. To John Coad's horror, the officers became suspicious of the prisoner calling himself Jo Haker, but after debating whether to take him with them, decided to make further enquiries when they returned to the shore. The master of the ship, however, fearing he would lose more prisoners and some of the cash commission he would receive for every rebel delivered alive to the plantations in Jamaica, weighed anchor as fast as he could and sailed out of Weymouth before the Sheriff's officers could return. It appears that the day after the ship left harbour, the authorities came for John Coad, but by then it was too late.

Still weak from his wounds and the long months of imprisonment John Coad was now drawing upon the last ounces of his faith and strength to keep him going through the terrible voyage which was about to start. Much has been written about the shocking conditions on the slave ships which plied the Atlantic from Africa to the West Indies, but those on this voyage were almost beyond description and certainly as bad for the rebel prisoners incarcerated in the hold. There were 99 men battened beneath hatches in the small hold where they could not lie down without lying on each other, and were not allowed on deck. A large container was set in the middle of the hold for sanitary purposes, and it goes without saying that within a very short time, the ship was infected with all sorts of diseases described as smallpox, fever and a plague which produced 'frightful blotches'. Some 22 prisoners died during the voyage, together with several of the crew, including the master's mate, and a number of free passengers making their way to Jamaica. The shocking voyage ended six weeks and three days later when the ship anchored off Port Royal, and the prisoners were put ashore. Their appearance was such that many of the townspeople who had come down to meet the ship took pity on the survivors and provided them with fresh water and food. The men were housed in a stable for some ten days and, although confined at night, they were given the freedom to walk about the town during the day.

John Coad remained in Jamaica until 1690, and appears to have been fairly well treated. At one time he served as an overseer on a plantation and continued in his trade as a carpenter. King James II was overthrown in 1688, but it was not until the summer of 1690 that pardons were brought to Jamaica and John Coad and his fellow rebels were given free passage home to England.

John Coad's long journey was not, however, without incident, involving violent storms, fear of attack from French privateers, and the ship was nearly lost on several occasions. England was at last sighted at four o'clock on the afternoon of Saturday, 22 November 1690, a little south of Plymouth. When the ship came near to Plymouth, John Coad suggested to the master that they should put into port because being alone the vessel could be in danger from French privateers operating in the English Channel. The master pointed out that it would cost £5 for a pilot to guide the ship into Plymouth and, as he was bound for London, he was not prepared to incur the expense or the delays that this would involve. However, the ship's timbers had seriously sprung during the recent storms and she was now leaking badly. John Coad, as an experienced carpenter, was able to convince the master that it was unlikely the vessel would reach London, and the owners would not be very pleased if she foundered on the way; it was much more sensible to spend £5 than lose the ship. The arguments must have lasted for some time because when the master finally made up his mind to put into port, the ship was off Dartmouth. Here the master fired a cannon to call out the Dartmouth pilot who brought with him a press gang looking for merchant seamen for the Royal Navy. Observing the dreaded press gang coming alongside, the sailors deserted their posts and took refuge in various parts of the vessel even though she was under full sail and close to land. Had it not been for the press gang helping to bring the ship about, she would have crashed onto the rocks and John Coad might not have made England alive after all.

Finally, two days later on 24 November 1690, the Stoford carpenter set foot on English soil, and in his own words, 'December 4th got home, found my wife and three sons living, but in a poor low condition.'

# JAMES MARTIN AND THE FLOOD OF '94

It rained hard continuously across the West Country for three days on Saturday, Sunday and Monday 10, 11 and 12 November 1894, and although there was a brief respite on Tuesday, it poured through the night until midday Wednesday when it finally stopped. Most of the rivers overflowed their banks and the Somerset Levels were under water.

The River Parrett overflowed the embankments at Langport, and within hours, Bow Street was under five feet of water. Boats were rowed through the main street, and in parts the water was deep enough for a large keel-boat to be sailed into Cheapside. No one could recall such flooding and, for the first time in living memory, the ground floor of the Langport Arms Hotel was under two feet of water. The gasworks was put out of action for several days, and rail traffic on the Yeovil to Taunton line was brought to a complete standstill for two days with over seven feet of floodwater across part of the permanent way. Of all the Somerset towns and villages affected by the severe floods, Langport suffered the most; thankfully there was no loss of life in the town. Even so, the floods were causing chaos across the county; the lower parts of Frome were inundated, several streets in Wells were under water, and for a day, the city was almost cut off from the rest of Somerset. At Taunton the River Tone rose rapidly, and in Tangier over 100 houses were flooded; for a time the county town lost all its rail communications. The city of Bath was severely affected with houses and businesses on the banks of the River Avon being flooded and thousands of residents were unable to leave their homes due to the flooding of the lower parts of the houses.

The special reporter for *Pulman's Weekly News* described the moorland above Langport as presenting a sight 'of imposing grandeur, the water extending miles beyond the range of vision'.

However, floods or not, carrier James Martin was not going to be prevented from carrying out his rounds and so he set out from Yeovil with his horse and cart to deliver gloves, groceries and drapery to the villages around South Petherton. He got as far as Shores Bridge (now replaced by a modern bridge on the A303), but as he drove the heavily-laden cart through the flooded road leading to the bridge, the current swept the feet from under the horse, the cart tipped and for a moment the animal and vehicle were caught in the torrent. Trees and a bank prevented the horse and cart, together with occupants – for there was a passenger by name of Clarke en route to Shepton

Beauchamp – from being swept into the river and drowned there and then. Even so, the unfortunate horse did not survive but James Martin and his companion clung to the wagon and shouted and prayed for help.

The event was witnessed by George Wines who raised the alarm and with his employer at Bridge House, Mr Blake, and a Mr Jones, began the rescue operations. First they tried to drive another horse and cart into the flood but were driven back by the violence of the water. Then Mr Blake bravely waded chest high into the swirling water, and finally succeeded in throwing a rope to the two cold, tired and desperate men, and pulled them to safety. James Martin was in a state of complete exhaustion, and although he was supplied with hot drinks had to be driven to the Bell Inn, in South Petherton where he slowly recovered following the ministrations of the landlady.

The valuable horse was drowned and the contents of the cart completely ruined – as was James Martin's one-horse-and-cart transport enterprise.

# DEATHS ON THE LINE

The Great Western Railway Company's passenger train was approaching Marston Magna from the Yeovil direction early in the morning of 25 January 1866 when out of the winter gloom, the driver, Edward Johnson, saw a dark shape appear on line about 50 yards ahead. He shut off the steam, put the engine in reverse and blew the whistle. Too late, the train which had been travelling at over 40 miles an hour, smashed into the shape, which he now saw to be a trolley carrying several lengths of rail, and a quarter of a mile up the line the locomotive finally came to a stop. Driver Johnson inspected the front of his engine, but finding little damage, went on his way. One of the passengers was Mr John Rodber, the permanent way inspector for the track between Yeovil and Sparkford, who got out and ran back down the line to find out what had happened. He found the trolley completely destroyed, several lengths of rail scattered along the track and two men bending over a third who was stretched out moaning on the ground. He identified the injured man as one of his gangers, James Brown, who had suffered two horribly broken legs. Meanwhile, Levi Willie, the ganger in charge of the working party, had disappeared. Two wooden hurdles were quickly found and the injured man was taken to his nearby home, where he died the following morning. This was now a possible case of manslaughter, and a warrant was out for Levi Willie's arrest. Following the Magistrates' hearing on the fugitive's surrender several days later, he was formally committed for trial at the forthcoming Somerset Assizes.

Levi Willie, was brought before the Judge, Mr Baron Channell, at the Assize Court at Taunton in the following March, charged with the manslaughter of James Brown. Following the evidence of the engine driver Edward Johnson, the next witness, James Parsons, described the accident. He stated that, together with the prisoner, John Marsh and James Brown, he was helping to remove rails from the trolley for the repair of several lengths of line about ½ a mile from Marston Magna station. Three of the gangers were on the trolley when they heard, and then saw, the train approaching and jumped for their lives. James Parsons had managed to get well clear and turning back, saw James Brown standing fairly close to the track. When the engine hit the trolley the two rails left unloaded had flown off and one had struck James Brown below his knees knocking him several yards. The injured man had cried out, 'My legs are off!' before lapsing into semi-consciousness. The witness stated that Levi Willie had run up, and putting his hand on the injured man, said, 'Poor Brown is dead, and I must leave.' John Marsh had shouted, 'Don't leave us in this mess!' to which the prisoner replied, 'I am bound to go.' And with this he had run away towards Marston Station. James Parsons went on to say that the trolley had been put on the line at Marston Station at about a quarter to seven village time and he had pointed out to the prisoner that the up-train would be due before long; Willie had looked at his watch and replied that there was plenty of time. Fellow ganger John Marsh corroborated his colleague's statement.

Dr Williams of Sherborne told the court that both of the deceased's legs had been badly broken below the knee; he had given stimulants and had watched him. Early the next morning James Brown had asked for both his legs to be amputated, which operation was carried out, but half an hour later the patient died. Dr Williams stated that if the amputation had not taken place, death would still have occurred within another day.

Counsel for the Great Western Railway Company read the regulations to be observed when work was being carried out on the track. No trolley or other vehicle was allowed on the line within fifteen minutes of a train being due, and a man with a red flag by day and red light by night, must be positioned as a signalman, one mile from the place of work. This had not been done in this case.

Mr John Rodbard, testified that he was the inspector of the permanent way between Yeovil and Sparkford and had ten gangers under him. He considered Levi Willie to be the best of them and he was a very steady and careful man.

Mr Edlin, for the prisoner, stated that his client admitted that he had not set a signalman because he was one man short, and he believed that he had enough time for the work, however, his watch had deceived him by being twenty minutes late. He also considered that the deceased had plenty of time to escape but had put himself in danger. Mr Edlin stated that Willie was thirty-five years of age, had been in the employ of the company for six years, and was a sober, honest, hardworking and well-conducted man.

The jury found Levi Willie guilty, but with a strong recommendation for mercy, and the Judge sentenced him to six months' hard labour.

Four and a half years later, seventy-three-year-old Benjamin Horton took the first and last train ride of his life to Weymouth on Tuesday 2 August 1870. Benjamin was a door-keeper at Messrs Cockey's Frome foundry and was well liked and respected by his workmates and the congregation of the parish where he had been the verger. The story of the last train ride was recounted at the inquest into the death of Benjamin Horton held in the Pen

Mill Hotel, Yeovil, on the following day.

One hundred and fifty employees of the Frome foundry had spent their annual outing at Weymouth, and after a pleasant day, had left for home on the 6.30pm return excursion train. At about 7.30pm, the train stopped at Yetminster station and Benjamin Horton had got out (possibly to use the lavatory), leaving behind in his compartment, his hat, walking stick and a crab. Unfortunately, the stop was brief and as the train pulled away Benjamin Horton was seen running along the platform, but was unable to get back into his compartment. Ignoring calls from the Yetminster station staff, the elderly man set off along the railway line in the direction of Yeovil.

At about eight o'clock, George Edgar was driving the 6.50pm Weymouth to Bristol excursion train on the up-line through the Bradford cutting, about two miles from Yeovil, when he saw a man walking towards the town along the opposite down-line. Driver Edgar sounded his whistle but, to his horror, the man suddenly stepped across onto the upline and into the path of his engine. There was no chance to apply the brakes, and the man was struck by the excursion's locomotive. After bringing the train to a halt, Driver Edgar, his fireman and the guard, ran back to find the badly mangled body of an elderly man. The corpse was placed in an empty compartment and conveyed to Yeovil Pen Mill Station where it was laid in the porter's rest room.

The following morning, the body was identified by a fellow worker from Messrs Cockey's foundry as Benjamin Horton, and following the inquest verdict of 'killed by an excursion train in the line between Yetminster and Yeovil', the deceased was taken home to Frome that evening.

No one could understand why Benjamin Horton had stepped into the path of the Bristol excursion train, except that as he had never been on a train before, he may have become confused when he heard the whistle.

# THE FIGHT AT PYE CORNER

Village rivalries are probably as old as villages and, though they sometimes flared into fisticuffs with bloody noses and bruises, rarely was the outcome fatal. Sadly, one such encounter proved deadly for twenty-six-year-old William Holland of West Coker.

Members of the Odcombe Friendly Society held their annual Club Dinner at the Pye Corner Inn near the village, on 7 September 1846: the food was good, there was plenty to drink and the Odcombe men were in high spirits. However, there were a number of West Coker men drinking at the inn, and towards the end of the evening quarrelling broke out between the villagers and the West Coker contingent departed. Shortly after, at about ten o'clock, the Odcombe men began to disperse, but as they left, fighting broke out. Luke Ash, a draper living in Odcombe, would later describe how, 'as fast as the Odcombe men came out, the Coker men knocked them down, took away some of their hats and ran down the lane towards Coker.'

However, the West Coker men were outnumbered by the Odcombe men, who drove them along the lane under a hail of stones and with blows from large sticks. It was during this barrage that William Holland was felled by a large stone thrown at him from less than 9 feet by Thomas Penall from Odcombe, and was carried semi-conscious home to West Coker.

The following day, William Holland's condition was causing concern and despite the attentions of Mr Frederick Nisbet, the Yeovil Poor Law Union surgeon responsible for West Coker, he died on 26 September; four days later, William was buried in the village churchyard.

Thomas Penall, together with three other Odcombe men, Henry Brake, George Chant and William Frampton, were arrested, charged with the manslaughter of William Holland and lodged in the County Gaol to await trial.

Six months later, the four men appeared at the Somerset Spring Assizes. Witnesses described the running fight, how William Holland had been felled by the heavy stone thrown by Thomas Penall, and how the other three defendants had been the ringleaders of the Odcombe men. Surgeon Nisbet, whose evidence was crucial to the prosecution, told how he had seen the

...deceased at his house at West Coker on the morning of 8 September. I examined his skull. I found a large external wound over the left eyebrow, and a fracture of the bone corresponding with it, a portion of which was depressed and lying on the surface of the brain. The wound appeared to be made by some heavy blunt body, and was such a one as was likely to be produced by a stone. It was a very serious and dangerous wound. The symptoms were those of concussion of the brain. It occurred to me that the operation of trepanning (cutting a hole in the skull) must be performed at some time or the other, should he live long enough. The operation is not a proper one to be performed without symptoms of concussion and depression existing together. On Wednesday I judged it safe to proceed with the operation and I performed it with Mr Sharland assisting me. There was scarcely any improvement subsequent to the operation; after the third day he did improve for a short time and I had strong hopes that he would recover but he died on 26 September. A post-mortem examination was made the day after. The cause of death was an abscess of considerable size deep in the substance of the brain, and also an inflamed state of the membranes of the brain. These were quite sufficient to cause death. I attributed the abscess and inflammation to the missile which caused the depression of the skull and destroyed the vitality of the part. In my judgement, the operation was correct and proper.

Defence counsel, Mr Edwards, believed that the West Coker men had started the fight, disputed the evidence that Penall had thrown the stone, and suggested that had the operation been carried out before the inflammation had commenced, William Holland would probably have recovered.

In his summing up the Judge, Mr Justice Cresswell, pointed out that when two bodies were fighting one and all of them were equally responsible for any of the injuries caused and it was not a question for the jury to consider whether Penall threw the stone, or whether either of the other persons threw it because which ever it was, the others were aiding and abetting and consequently equally liable. Had one man out of the large body only thrown a stone, the case would have been different, but as it was, there was a large body of men who were all throwing stones and exciting each other on, and the prisoners at the bar appeared, from the evidence, to be the principal instigators of the fray.

After some deliberation the jury return verdicts of guilty.

In sentencing the four men, the Judge stated that because they had been in gaol already for six months he sentenced them to one calendar month's hard labour.

# A HORRID MURDER IN BATH

The two shots and cries of 'murder!', which rang out in the clear moon-light early hours of Sunday, 27 January 1828, brought night-watchmen running to the fashionable 16 Marlborough Buildings in the city of Bath, the house of eighty-year-old Mrs Elizabeth Coxe. After gaining access through the back of the house, the watchmen found signs of robbery, and in the kitchen discovered the body of forty-two-year-old lady's maid, Maria Bagnall, with her throat cut lying in a pool of blood, and a large bludgeon lying by her side.

At ten o'clock on the Sunday morning, G.H. Tugwell Esq, Mayor and Coroner of Bath, summoned a jury for the inquest on the deceased Maria Bagnall, and with 21 jurymen proceeded to 16 Marlborough Buildings where they examined the body and inspected every room. On their return to the Guildhall, the examination of witnesses began and the events of the early morning were revealed.

The first witness was Richard Gillham, the butler, who stated that had been in the service of Mrs Coxe for sixteen months, and his wife was the cook. They slept in one of the garret rooms, and this morning he had woken up and heard the clock strike two o'clock. About ten minutes later the witness recalled hearing some sounds in the house below as if some one was trying to break open the door of the closet on the attic landing where his mistress kept her valuable plate. Without waking his wife or putting on his clothes, Gillham stated that he had gone down the garret stairs, which were lit by the bright moonlight, but found the door at the bottom fastened from the other side and he could not open it. At this moment he thought he heard the bolt to the closet thrown back and, retreating back to the bedroom, he took three pistols from a carpet-bag, loaded two with powder and ball, and the third with powder only. The butler stated that he had put on his morning clothes and went back down the stairs. Once again he found the door fastened and think-ing he could hear someone behind it, fired one of the pistols through the door. Although there was no sound from the other side, the door remained fastened. Returning to the garret, Gillham stated that he fired one of the pistols out of a back window, and another at the front, calling for the watch and shouting 'murder!' Hearing the sound of rattles, and the watchmen knocking on the locked street door, the witness shouted down that they were locked in, there were thieves in the house and to go around to the back way.

Gillham recalled how he had gone back down the garret stairs and succeeded in forcing open the door just as one of the watchmen arrived on the attic landing. After checking to ensure that Mrs Coxe was unharmed in her room on the attic floor, he had accompanied the watchman back down to the main rooms. Here they met another watchman who told them that there was a woman lying dead in the kitchen.

The witness described how he had found Maria Bagnall lying on her face, quite dead, with her throat cut and a large quantity of blood on the stone floor. He had tried to lift her but she was quite cold, and in doing so he noticed a large bludgeon beside the corpse. Gillham explained that the blood found on his clothes must have come from his kneeling down to lift the dead lady's maid.

Gillham described how, with one of the watchmen, he had examined the rooms, and found drawers pulled out and turned over. The cellaret in the drawing room had been broken open and its contents of wine and one of gin appeared to have been consumed and the empty bottles left on the table. Near the kitchen door they found the silver tea urn on the floor and a bundle containing a pelisse belonging to his wife and his greatcoat. The butler stated that from his examination of the rooms, nothing seemed to have been taken from the house.

Going into the cellar, they found a basket containing a leg of lamb and a dressed shoulder, together with some loaves of bread, all of which had been taken from the larder. The back door seemed to have been forced from the frame, and there were impressions of some instrument between the door and the outside frame. Gillham stated that he had not secured the door last evening as the servant Ann Spackman generally closed it.

Returning with a watchman to the attic landing, the butler checked the plate chest and found it secure. He also found a gimlet on the floor which appeared to have been bored into the door of the garret stairs above the latch to prevent it being raised. Gillham stated that this must have flown out when he forced the door open, and he gave it to the watchman.

In concluding his evidence, Richard Gillham disclosed that he been given notice to quit Mrs Coxe's service as a result of his marriage to the cook.

Jane Gillham followed her husband onto the witness stand, and confirmed that she had been married for five months. She had lived and served Mrs Coxe as cook for eleven years. They had gone to bed at about eleven o'clock, and she remembered being woken by her husband getting out of bed, saying that he thought he had heard someone in the house. Jane Gillham thought she could hear something like a whispering noise and then the shots were fired and her husband called for the watch. She had gone down the stairs with her husband and the watchman, and saw the body of Maria Bagnall lying on the floor. The witness stated that they were on very good terms with the dead woman, and on going to bed last night they had met her going down the stairs and wished her a good night.

Ann Spackman, the seventy-year-old servant, testified that she had been in Mrs Coxe's service for nearly thirteen years, and that Maria Bagnall was on good terms with her fellow servants. The witness stated that she occupied one of the garret rooms and the Gillhams another. She had gone to bed at about ten o'clock, and she heard Gillham and his wife come up to bed shortly after. The shots had woken her up and Ann Spackman stated that she had gone down to Mrs Coxe's room and stayed with her mistress. The aged servant said that she had never heard Richard Gillham and Maria Bagnall quarrel about a new servant coming to the house. She confirmed that she sometimes fastened the back door, but had not done so last night.

Watchman Charles Burlington was called and stated that at about half past two o'clock he had been on duty in The Crescent when he heard the sound of shots and the cry of 'watch' and 'murder' coming from 16 Marlborough Buildings. He had 'sprung' his rattle and hurried to the house. Burlington recalled that the street door could not be opened but a man had called down from the upper part of the building stating that he had been shut in, there were thieves in the house and entreated him to go around the back way. Several other members of the watch had now arrived, and together they had gone around by the Weston Lane, through the wicket gate and into the field behind Marlborough Buildings. They saw an open gate in the garden wall which they took to be that of No. 16, and going through found an open back door into the cellar. Watchman Burlington and his companions went in and up some stairs onto a landing where a candle was burning in a plated candlestick. Leaving the other watchmen to explore the lower floors, the witness continued up the main stairs and as he called out for the occupants a man's voice shouted that they were fastened in. Arriving at the attic landing, he heard something fall and the door to the garret stairs burst open to reveal Gillham, the butler, wearing a nightcap and his day clothes. Watchman Burlington saw a gimlet on the floor and near the door was a white-handled case knife which he picked up and on later examination was found to be clean. A tall woman then joined them, whom Gillham said was his wife, and they went back down the stairs to be told that a dead woman had been found in the kitchen. The watchman recalled the scene in the kitchen but he was certain that Richard Gillham had not touched the body.

James Dawkins who described himself as 'a patrol of the city', was the next witness. He recounted hearing the reports of the pistols and the shouts of murder, and on his arrival a 16 Marlborough Buildings he found three watchmen at the street door. Dawkins accompanied the watchmen, and on entering the house he had gone down to the kitchen with two of the watch where they found the woman's body. Her throat had been cut and she was lying in a large pool of congealed blood with her cap nearby on the floor. There was a large bludgeon by the side of the corpse, but a search of the kitchen revealed no other weapon. Dawkins stated that he was present when Gillham came into the kitchen, but he could not say whether he had touched the body or lifted it.

Night Constable William Morey testified that he had examined the rooms with Richard Gillham, and when they reached the garret door he had produced the gimlet and showed how it had been fastened in a hole above the latch. Morey also noted the bullet hole in the door and the mark on the opposite wall where the ball had struck. The butler had given him the gimlet.

The last witness, Thomas King of Brock Street, surgeon, recalled that at about three o'clock that morning he had been called by a watchman to 16 Marlborough Buildings where he saw the body of Maria Bagnall lying on the kitchen floor face downwards. The surgeon found that the dead woman had received a severe blow on the head, another over the right eye, and her throat was cut so severely that the wound extended to the spine and the head was nearly severed from the body. This would have caused instant death. He noted that the right hand was much bruised and the thumb and middle finger were badly lacerated. Mr King found the body quite stiff, the blood coagulated, and in his opinion, the murder must have been committed about three hours earlier at around midnight. In concluding his evidence, the surgeon stated that he visited Mrs Coxe professionally and had heard her say that the deceased and Gillham and his wife did not like each other.

Following the examination of the witnesses, the jury returned a verdict of 'wilful murder against some person or persons unknown'.

On Monday 28 January, advertisements were placed in the local newspapers for information leading to the conviction of the murderer or murderers — £100 by the Mayor of Bath and £50 by the Parish of Walcot. Several suspects were brought in for questioning and then released. However, to the City Magistrates' officers there were aspects of the case which threw suspicion on the butler, Richard Gillham. Some of the drawers had been opened and ransacked, but on examination they had not been opened by pick locks, the usual instrument used by burglars, and no items taken; the door to the garret stairs was so flimsy it could have been burst open with little force and it had been opened before the watchman could confirm the butler's statement that the gimlet was securing the latch; the butler had told William Morey, the night constable, that he had locked and barred the back door but at the inquest he said that the servant had done so; on examining the door Morey found no sign of the bar being forced, and it appeared that the staples, which were fixed inside had been forced from the inside; with the street door locked and no sign of external forcing of the only back door how had the robbers entered the house? Furthermore, the breeches, shirt and waistcoat worn by Gillham were bloodstained and the watchman Burlington had testified that he had not seen him touch the corpse. A clasp knife, which appeared to have been recently washed, was found in a drawer in Gillham's room.

Richard Gillham was taken in for questioning late on Monday but despite the questioning continuing on Tuesday, the evidence was still insufficient to bring charges. The Magistrates were not prepared to give up, and on Wednesday he was brought before the Mayor and subjected to a three-hour interrogation. On this occasion Gillham was asked whether he was in possession of any property in Bath, other than what he had at 16 Marlborough Buildings, and he replied none whatever.

Later on Wednesday, information came into the Mayor's hands that Gillham had a large quantity of goods stored in 6 William's Place, a house occupied by an ostler called Roberts, at the back of Northampton Street. Two city officers were despatched to the address and finding the information to be correct, removed three hampers, three boxes, a basket and a large saucepan to the Guildhall. When opened, the hampers and boxes were found to contain 17 bottles of wine, assorted china, earthen and tinware, candles and chamber candlesticks, knives and forks, fire irons, a patent corkscrew and various other articles, much of which was identified as the property of Mrs Elizabeth Coxe.

The Mayor then sent the two officers to the city gaol to ask Gillham once again whether he had any property elsewhere in Bath, and when he denied it, the trap was sprung. At noon on Thursday, the butler was brought to the Guildhall for re-examination, and the hampers and boxes placed so that he would see them as he entered the room. At first he showed no emotion, but as the hampers were opened one by one and their contents displayed, Gillham became distraught, almost fainted and had to be revived with a large cup of water. On being questioned on the ownership of the goods and cautioned by the Mayor not to answer if he did not wish to, the butler remained silent and was taken back to his cell.

The following morning, John Bourne, the keeper of the city gaol visited Richard Gillham and found him very distressed. Following a long discussion, the Rev. William Marshall, the gaol chaplain was sent for, and he spent several hours with the butler during the rest of the day praying, reading from the Bible, and exhorting his repentance and reconciliation with God.

At eight o'clock on Saturday morning, the Rev. Marshall again visited Gillham who made a full confession of the murder of Maria Bagnall. He disclosed that there had been repeated quarrels with the lady's maid following her comments that she believed he was stealing from Mrs Coxe. On the fatal night she had accused him again and finished by saying, 'I've enough to hang you.' Gillham stated that he had struck her with a stick and cut her throat.

The Mayor was informed immediately, and at ten o'clock, in company with Mr George, the Town Clerk, he arrived at the gaol, and took the following confession of Richard Gillham:

On the night of Saturday 26 January, I and my wife went up stairs together to go to bed. On our way we met Maria Bagnall and on passing her, at about eleven o'clock, we wished her goodnight. After I had gone upstairs, I told my wife that I must go down again as my bowels were disordered. I accordingly went downstairs and went into my pantry, from which I took a stick, which I had in my possession, having cut it myself some months since. I met her by the kitchen door, when I struck her a blow on the head. I repeated my blows till she fell. I continued striking her, she at the time screaming out that she would have me hanged. By some means, I know not how, I fell on her. She continued screaming. I knelt upon her body, and taking my pocket knife from my waistcoat pocket, cut her throat with it; leaving the body in the state in which it was found. I then shut the knife, and put it into my waist coat pocket. On the following day I took it from my pocket, and placed it in a table drawer in my room. I then placed by her side the bludgeon which was found there. The stick I used was neither so large or so large as that bludgeon. I cut it up in the morning and lighted the fire with it. I took a purse out of the pocket of the deceased, it contained only a few halfpence, which I put in my waistcoat pocket. I then washed my hands and went upstairs to my room, when my wife inquired what was the matter I told her to say nothing about it to the old woman, Nanny, and that she was to say I had not been downstairs at all, but I had gone to bed before her. I then went downstairs again, and took with me the silver tea-urn, which I placed on the stairs where it was found. I had previously opened the cellaret, plate cupboard and drawers. Part of the wine and the spirits I took down stairs, and threw away. As nearly as I can tell, it must have been about ten minutes after eleven o'clock when I murdered her. It was with the pocket knife alone that I inflicted the wound in her throat. My wife knew nothing at all of the murder until after the pistols were fired, and the watchmen had come into the house.

By the time he had finished dictating his confession, Richard Gillham was in a state of collapse, and his hand was shaking so badly that he could not sign the document. However, the Mayor and Town Clerk signed as witnesses.

At noon, Gillham was brought before the City Magistrates at the Guildhall, and sent for trial at the forthcoming Somerset Spring Assizes, charged with the murder of Maria Bagnall. The prisoner was conveyed back to the gaol through hostile crowds, and shortly after five o'clock the following Sunday morning he was taken by two of the Mayor's officers to Shepton Mallet Gaol to await his trial.

Richard Gillham from Taplow in Buckinghamshire, was twenty-five-years old and described as being about 5 feet 8 inches tall, with light brown curling hair, large mouth, small grey eyes and rather heavy eye brows, his gait was rather awkward 'from being what is usually termed "in-kneed".'

The forty-two-year-old lady's maid, Maria Bagnall, a native of Hammersmith, had been two years in the service of Mrs Coxe, and was buried in Walcot burial ground on 30 January 1828. A Mr Gahagan, sculptor, residing in Bath, made a detailed drawing and model of the dead woman on the morning of the 27th, and which was said to 'be remarkably accurate'.

On Tuesday, 8 April 1828, Richard Gillham stood before Mr Justice Littledale at the Assizes in Taunton, charged with the murder of Maria Bagnall and pleaded 'not guilty'. Before opening the prosecution's case, counsel for the Crown, Mr Gunning, referred to the exhibition in Taunton of a model representing Maria Bagnall with her throat cut and the murderer standing over her, and cautioned the jury against being led away by any prejudices they might have as a consequence.

The trial last the whole of the day, during which the details of the case as presented at the inquest and subsequent hearings were recalled and recounted. However, counsel for Gillham concentrated their defence on his confession, the circumstances under which it had been obtained, and whether this had been the result of undue influence brought on him by the Rev. Marshall.

In his summing up, the Judge observed that there had been much discussion whether the confession of the prisoner could be received in evidence but this he would leave to be considered by the twelve Judges should he have any subsequent doubt. However, in his opinion, the confession could be received in evidence.

The jury took just five minutes to return a verdict of 'guilty', and Mr

Justice Littledale passed the sentence of death on Richard Gillham. The Judge then decided to respite the execution until 4 June, in order to leave the question of the admissibility of the confession to be decided by the twelve Judges of the Court of Exchequer Chamber, and Gillham was taken to Ilchester Gaol to await his fate.

On Saturday, 3 May, the twelve Judges met in London to hear the arguments relating to Richard Gillham's confession. The principal point presented by his counsel was that after his arrest he was greatly depressed, and the chaplain of the gaol had so strongly worked upon 'his religious and temporal hopes and fears' that he had been induced to confess his guilt which he had previously strongly denied. Several cases were cited and quoted at great length, which Gillham's counsel believed set precedents to be applied in this case and would mean the confession should be set aside as inadmissable. At three o'clock in the afternoon, the Judges decided to adjourn the hearing for a week. On the following Saturday the twelve Judges considered at length the legal question of whether any hope or fear had been held out to Gillham which could induce him to confess what was not true and to declare himself guilty of a crime he had not committed. With the conclusion of the submissions, the Judges announced after half an hour's consultation that the 'confession was admissable evidence against the prisoner, and consequently the conviction against him was according to law'. Richard Gillham would hang on 4 June.

On Tuesday 10 June 1828 the *Bath and Cheltenham Gazette* reported that:

Richard Gillham underwent the dreadful sentence of the law on Wednesday morning on the platform erected at the top of the lodge of Ilchester Gaol. On the day of his execution he made a full confession of his guilt to the Rev. Mr Valentine, the chaplain, and to Mr Hardy, the gaoler, and said he 'was goaded on to commit the act from the unkindness and ill-treatment he had experienced for the last nine months from the deceased Maria Bagnall, and that if he had not taken her life, he most certainly should have taken his own'. At the hour of four in the morning his cell was unlocked and he was conducted to his day room, where he continued praying until eight o'clock, at which time the Chaplain arrived, full prayers were then read in the chapel, at which all the prisoners attended,and at the conclusion, the Sacrament was administered to Gillham. He at this time seemed much depressed, and wept often. At half past nine he was conducted in the usual way to the scaffold. On ascending the ladder he faltered, and was supported on the platform, there he joined in prayer about five minutes, and the Chaplain then retired. The executioner, after tying him to the fatal beam, proceeded to put the cap over his eyes; but he having expressed a wish to have it removed, as he said, to see a person he expected in the crowd beneath, who had lived next door to him, but not seeing him there, the cap was again replaced, and at twenty-two minutes before ten the drop fell, and the world closed on the wretched culprit for ever. After hanging the usual time, his body was delivered to the order of Mr Norman, surgeon of this city, for dissection, it arrived at the United Hospital that evening. The concourse of the people at the execution was very small owing probably to the witness of the morning. On Thursday morning a notice was posted on the door of the United Hospital, stating that admission would be given to all members of the profession to inspect the body. The dissection of the body has been turned to the best advantages for public utility, all members of the medical profession in the city were allowed to be present, and Mr Norman, Mr Soden, Mr Browne and Mr Gore demonstrated in that judicious manner, which could not fail to impress on the minds of their auditors the most valuable information. Mr Crook, Phrenological Lecturer from London, has taken a cast of the head, and the body, we understand, will be preserved in a skeleton form in the theatre of the hospital.

On Tuesday, 27 May 1828, the same newspaper had reported that 'The wife of Gillham, the murderer was recently delivered of a daughter at Cheltenham.'

# IF ONLY THEY HAD BEEN ABLE TO SWIM

The beautiful little church of St Andrew, Brympton D'Evercy, near Yeovil, with its unusual bellcot, stands close to the equally beautiful Brympton House, one of the finest in Somerset. The name of the collection of Hamstone buildings which form this small settlement, derives from the D'Evercy family who were lords of the manor in the thirteeth century and who, with their successors, lie buried in and around the church. There are many brass memorials in the south transept to the Clive-Ponsonby-Fane family who owned the Brympton estate in the eighteenth, nineteenth and twentieth centuries, including one to sixteen-year-old Eleanor Ponsonby who was drowned in the lake of Brympton House on 3 September 1878. This is her sad tale.

Laughing and chattering, three young ladies ran across the terrace of Brympton House and down to the lake where the small rowing boat was moored against the bank. 'I'll row,' called out Caroline Gore as she scrambled aboard followed by sisters Margaret and Eleanor Ponsonby. Could anyone think of a better way of enjoying that early September afternoon in 1878 than a trip on the lake in the splendid surroundings of Brympton House.

We are not told whether Caroline Gore was a proficient oarswoman, but somehow the boat ran against the bank at the place where the feeder stream flowed into the lake. The girls tried to push the vessel away from the bank, but as they did so the bow dipped, and water poured over the side. The laughter turned to screams of fear as the boat rapidly filled and then capsized, tipping the occupants into the lake.

John Bullen, the butler, was going about his daily duties in the house when he heard the screams, and rushing out to the terrace saw, to his horror, the boat turn over and sink. He raced across the lawn, and although he could not swim, jumped into the lake and waded out to the rescue. Gardener, John Redward, had also heard the screams, and came running in time to help the butler drag Caroline Gore and Margaret Ponsonby onto the bank. John Bullen then went back to help Eleanor, but although he waded out as far as he could, she was out of reach, and the gallant butler who could not swim, was almost out of his depth. There was no way he could rescue the drowning girl, and he was forced to return to shallower water. Alas, John Redward was also a non-swimmer, and both men watched helplessly as Eleanor disappeared into the dark waters. By now the household were rushing down to

104

the lake, but it was too late. Eleanor Ponsonby had drowned.

The body was recovered later in the afternoon and on the morning of 4 September, the Coroner held his inquest at Brympton House. Miss Margaret Ponsonby and Miss Caroline Gore gave their evidence in a private room, and the jury also heard from the butler and the gardener on the unsuccessful attempt to rescue Eleanor. A verdict of 'accidentally drowned' was returned and the jury gave their fees to the Yeovil Hospital.

Eleanor's grave is in the northeast corner of the churchyard, together with those of other members of her family, all of which lie north/south and not the usual east/west.

In the churchyard of St Andrew's lies young Thomas Old, a glover, who ten years later went to Weymouth on Bank Holiday Monday, 6 August 1888. Shortly after he arrived, Thomas went down to the beach and hired a canoe. The boatman warned him not to go beyond the pier, but being a daring young fellow, Thomas paddled on and on. The captain of the yacht *Kitty*, cruising about a mile off shore, suddenly noticed someone struggling in the water and altered course to assist. On reaching the spot all he found was an empty canoe and a man's hat bobbing on the surface of the sea – of the struggling figure there was no sign. The canoe was towed ashore and the name and address of the hirer was established: Thomas Old of Brympton, near Yeovil. Six days later, Thomas Old's body was discovered by a boatman taking a fishing party to Portland. How he came to drown was never established, but it was suggested at the inquest that Thomas may have tried to stand up in the canoe and fell out because canoes could be notoriously unstable craft to the unwary. His brother told the inquest that he did not think Thomas had been out in a canoe before and was not used to boating. A verdict of 'found drowned' was returned and the body of twenty-two year-old Thomas Old was brought back home and buried in the quiet churchyard of St Andrew's. His epitaph reads, 'Beginning to sink he cried Lord save me.' St Matthew xiv - 30.

# THE FATAL FIGHT AT THE QUEEN'S HEAD

The bar of the Queen's Head, Milborne Port, was warm and full of regulars at about six o'clock in the early evening of Tuesday 14 November 1843. The reason why glover George Hallett and fellow glover John Barter, went to fight was never established. There was, however, some bad blood between them, and when George Hallett's demand that John Barter tell him what he had being saying about him was ignored, the stage was set for the fatal events of the next few hours. Both men appeared eager for a fight, coats were taken off, and blows were exchanged. Twice George Hallett was knocked to the floor but on the third occasion the back of his head struck the edge of a settle as he crashed to the ground. This time George Hallett did not get up and lay unconscious in a pool of blood. Drinking stopped and as everyone crowded around the fallen glover, a John Lewis shouted out that he was dead. However, this announcement was premature and as consciousness returned, Thomas Biss, the burly ostler at the Queen's Head, lifted him up and carried George Hallett out to the bowling alley and sat him down against a beer barrel. Seeing that the glover was recovering, the ostler left and went about his other duties.

A few minutes later, Charles Field, one of the drinkers in the bar accompanied by Caroline Duffett, the landlord's servant girl, took George Hallett's coat out to the bowling alley where they found him still slumped against the barrel. Refusing Caroline's offer to clean up his face, George Hallett was helped to his feet, and supported by Charles Field, walked to the town pump and washed himself whilst his companion pumped the water. Stating that he was now all right, George Hallett wished Charles Field a goodnight, and walked up the street towards Sherborne.

Butcher Joseph Hockey was returning home to Henstridge from business in Sherborne, and as he walked through the cutting at Crackmore Hill at about 7.30 the same evening, he stumbled across the body of a man lying in the road. After establishing that the man was dead, he went for help and on the arrival of the constable of Milborne Port, the corpse was identified as George Hallett. Dirt, grass and leaves on the dead man's shoes suggested that he could have fallen from the top of the cutting.

The following day Milborne Port was awash with rumour and speculation, the details of the fight were recounted again and again, and wild accusations of foul play were being made, fuelled by the arrest of John Barter. On Thursday 16 November the Coroner, Mr Ashford opened the inquest into the death of George Hallett, and witnesses described to the 'most respectable jury' the events of the Tuesday evening. However, Surgeon Parsons of Wincanton informed the Coroner that he had not been able to carry out a full post-mortem, and the inquest was adjourned until noon on Tuesday 21 November.

The first witness was John Parsons who testified that at about seven o'clock on the evening in question John Barter, in company with his brother and three other men, had arrived at his beer shop and had stayed drinking until about half past eight when William Hayward came in and announced that George Hallett had been found dead. The witness stated that John Barter and his companions seemed very shocked and surprised by the news and left immediately.

Surgeon Parsons described the injuries: severe bruising over the right eye, lacerations behind the right ear, which could have been caused by a pebble or stone, a cut on the right arm and a graze on the right shin. There had been severe bleeding in the cranial cavity but no fractures. In the surgeon's opinion, the deceased had received a severe blow either from a fist or from a fall onto a hard surface sufficient to cause death. After receiving such a blow the deceased could have walked to the place where he was found.

William Pitman testified that early in the Wednesday morning he had gone to the top of the cutting immediately above the spot where George Hallett's body had lain, and found signs that someone had been walking by the edge and fallen through the brambles.

With all the testimonies presented, the Jury began their deliberation, but before reaching a verdict, they asked for the recall of Surgeon Parsons to whom they put the question whether 'the blow received at the Queens Head, when fighting, was the cause of death?' and to which he replied, 'I cannot say that it was.' The jury then announced that as there was no evidence to prove that the blow delivered by John Barter had caused George Hallett's death, their verdict would be 'found dead in the cutting in the turnpike road leading from Milborne Port to Sherborne on Tuesday evening 14th instant with a severe injury to the head'.

John Barter, who had been held in custody was released, and George Hallett was borne to his grave in Milborne Port churchyard on 22 November by his fellow glovers.

# TWO HUNTS AND A SURPRISING ESCAPE

Traffic thunders along the A303 London to Exeter road less than a mile from St Andrew's church, yet the small village of Compton Pauncefoot, with its backdrop of hills and woods, could be miles from the hurly burly of the twenty-first century. This pleasant fifteenth-century church with its spire, rare in South Somerset, sits beside a small village green accompanied by a splendid Georgian Rectory and an eighteenth-century manor house.

High on the inside north wall of the tower is a memorial to Robert Hunt and other members of the Hunt family who, for two centuries from 1630, owned the Manor of Compton Pauncefoot. Robert Hunt died in February 1679, aged about seventy-one years, and during his long life was a lawyer, Member of Parliament for Ilchester and Sheriff of Somerset. Although he was an active supporter of King Charles I during the Great Civil War, following the defeat of the Royalist cause he reconciled himself with the Parliament and was appointed Sheriff of Somerset in 1654.

In March 1655, a minor rebellion led by a veteran Royalist, John Penruddock, against the Commonwealth of Oliver Cromwell, broke out in Wiltshire. After occupying Salisbury, breaking open the gaol and releasing all the prisoners, the 300 rebels marched to Blandford where they proclaimed Charles II, King of England. Unfortunately for the rebels, the good folk of Dorset wanted nothing of this rebellion as the memories of the late Civil War were still fresh in their minds. Penruddock and his little army retreated west through Yeovil and Chard, until they were routed in a bloodless skirmish at South Molton. John Penruddock was captured with some of his followers, and was executed at Exeter on 16 May 1655. Another rebel officer, Captain Thomas Hunt, was sentenced to death by beheading and transported to Ilchester Gaol where he was given into the care of the Sheriff of Somerset his namesake, but no relation, Robert Hunt.

Captain Hunt's execution was fixed for the evening of 7 May, but the axe needed to remove his head was proving difficult to find. It had to have a blade of 11 inches to carry out the task, and implements of this size were not in plentiful supply. The problem in procuring the axe, and the time required to build the scaffold before the Shire Hall in the market-place at Ilchester, had now delayed the execution until Thursday 10 May.

On the Wednesday night, the eve of the execution, Captain Hunt was allowed a last visit from his two sisters, Marjorie and Elizabeth. They arrived at the gaol at about ten o'clock, and were shown to their brother's cell which he shared with two other prisoners. His two companions were absent during the visit, and alone with his sisters, a daring escape was put in hand. Captain Hunt quickly changed clothes with Marjorie, and then with Elizabeth went through the gaol, passing three door-keepers and the main gate guard, to freedom. Back in the cell, Marjorie placed her brother's cloak and hat on a chair and got into his bed. On their return, the captain's cellmates thought he was asleep and took to their beds.

Having parted from his sister, Captain Hunt found himself wandering alone in the vicinity of Ilchester as dawn broke but without any idea of where he was; he could also hear the great bell of the gaol begin to toll for his impending execution. Just as he began to lose hope of making an escape, the captain espied a collier coming along the road leading a packhorse loaded with coal. Still in female disguise, Captain Hunt hailed the collier and in the conversation which followed discovered his destination. Telling the collier that that he was travelling in the same direction, the lady managed to persuade him to allow 'her' to ride with the coal on the horse. During the journey, the collier's Royalist sympathies soon became apparent and the captain took a desperate chance and disclosed that he was an escaped rebel. As events proved, this chance encounter was to save Captain Hunt's life, and in company with his new found saviour, he rode across country to the collier's home on the edge of the lonely Somerset Levels.

The escape had now been discovered, Marjorie was arrested and confessed. Sister Elizabeth was also apprehended, and both ladies were lodged in Ilchester Gaol, where they remained without being brought to trial until their release two years later in 1657. On discovering Captain Hunt's escape the hue and cry was raised, and Parliamentary troops stationed in Ilchester were soon scouring the countryside. The collier, meanwhile, having reached home, barricaded the door, left the lamps unlit, and the two men took cover in a small upper chamber of the cottage, each with a loaded musket preparing to sell their lives dearly if discovered. Before long a sheriff's officer with a troop of mounted men clattered into the yard and hammering on the door demanded entrance. At first the collier and his wife made no sign, but as the shouting of the troopers became more threatening, the collier put his head out of the chamber window as if disturbed from sleep, and demanded an explanation for this uproar. The sheriff's officer bellowed that the party was in pursuit of a prisoner escaped from Ilchester Gaol disguised as a female, and as he had orders to search every house, his men would force their way in if necessary. The collier replied that he would open the door as soon as he could get a light, but pretended that he had lost the steel for the tinder box. As no one else had any means of producing light, the troopers were told that they must search the house in the dark. The sheriff's officer by now had lost his patience with the apparent ignorance of the collier, and calling out that it was useless to waste time here because the stupid fellow did not know his right hand from his left, galloped away with the party, to the inexpressible relief of the fugitive and his faithful friends.

Captain Hunt remained hidden in the collier's cottage, and when the hue and cry had calmed down, the collier helped him in his escape to France where he joined the exiled Charles II with whom he remained until returning to England at the Restoration some five years later. The name of the collier who saved the captain's life, and whether he was rewarded for the terrible risk he took for a stranger, remains one of history's secrets.

As for Sheriff Robert Hunt, the escape of his namesake was an obvious embarrassment, but, surprisingly, it did not affect the career of this widely respected man. He continued in the office of Sheriff of Somerset for another year, served the County and Ilchester in the Parliaments of 1659 and 1660, and for the last two decades of his life continued to play an active role in County government as a Magistrate and Deputy Lieutenant. He now lies with his kin in St Andrew's church, in the peaceful village of Compton Pauncefoot.

# UP BEFORE THE BENCH

On 21 February 1857 Anthony Wills, jun., appeared before the Magistrates in Crewkerne summoned by Henry Sweet for assault and battery. Both young men lived in Merriott and the incident arose from a quarrel about a bet on 10 February. There was a cross-summons in which Anthony Wills was the complainant. It appeared that Anthony was enjoying a dance in the club room at the Bell Inn when Henry Sweet repeatedly attempted to trip him up. Anthony remonstrated with Henry who ignored him and, in exasperation, Anthony pushed his tormentor aside, upon which Henry threatened to run a knife into his guts. Susan Easton, Anthony Wills' partner confirmed his statement, but Henry Sweet denied attempting to trip anyone, although he admitted threatening to use the knife. Mary Sweet, Henry's sister backed up her brother's evidence and said that Anthony Wills appeared determined to kick up a row. The Magistrates decided that Anthony Wills had started the trouble and appeared to have been of a quarrelsome temper at the time. The cross-summons against Henry Sweet was dismissed, and Anthony Wills was fined ten shillings plus costs.

In the same court Abel Norton, a butcher of Merriott, was charged with shooting at a hare on land belonging to Lord Hinton at Hinton St George. The witness was a Mr James, an employee of Lord Hinton, who recalled that on the previous 2 December he had been in a field on the estate and had seen Abel Norton and a boy enter the land, both carrying guns. A few minutes later he saw both fire at a sitting hare, which they missed, and the animal ran away. On being challenged by Mr James, the butcher and his companion departed hastily. The defendant strongly denied that he had fired and that it had been the boy who had tried to shoot the hare. The Magistrates were not persuaded and fined Abel Norton £2 plus costs.

William Palmer appeared before the same Bench summoned by William Staple for stealing an iron hoop worth two shillings on 19 February 1857; both defendant and complainant were coopers. William Staple stated that the hoop had been in his Crewkerne shop at nine o'clock on the morning in question but three hours later it had gone. William Palmer lived opposite and on going into his house William Staple saw the missing hoop being used by the defendant. Mr Palmer stated that both men had been in the habit of borrowing each others tools and on the morning concerned he was sharpening Mr Staple's saw as a neighbourly act. He had no quarrel with the cooper but he believed he was drunk at the time. The Magistrates dismissed the case, commenting that it was quite clear that William Palmer had never intended to steal the hoop and expressing their concern to William Staple at bringing the summons.

In July 1871 Herbert Southey, the son of the Rev. C.C. Southey of Kingsbury Episcopi, appeared at the County Petty Sessions in Yeovil summoned for damaging the roof of the cottage belonging to labourer Job Richards on the side of Ham Hill. Job stated that at about seven o'clock on the evening of 21 June he had arrived home from work and had seen a picnic party on the hill above his cottage. Several of the young gentlemen began to throw stones down from the hill and he saw the defendant Southey throw several large stones onto the roof of his cottage. The roof comprised wooded boards and one of the stones, which he estimated to weigh about 1lb broke through, causing two shillings' worth of damage. Another of the party had also thrown stones onto the roof but Job had been unable to find his name.

Witness Mr Samuel Davis, an elderly gentleman, stated that he had been one of the party on the hill. Some of them had gone onto a ledge overlooking the cottage, and he had remarked that when he had been a lad he had often amused himself by seeing how far he could throw a stone. Some of the young gentlemen took up some stones and began trying to 'pitch them into the chimney of the cottage but which they did not know at the time was inhabited'. None of the stones were as heavy as claimed by Job Richards. Mr Davis stated that he had not tried to stop the stone throwing because he had not thought it would cause harm or annoyance.

The Chairman of the Magistrates then suggested to the complainant that this had only been 'a foolish lark' and he felt sure that if he had spoken to Mr Southey properly and told him what damage had been done, he would willingly have paid the money. Job Richards replied that when he had approached Mr Southey and his friends they had threatened to roll him down the hill. He would not have taken out the summons if they had been civil to him, but they had not, and had called his house a pigsty. The Bench advised Southey to be careful where he threw stones, and ordered him to pay a fine of one shilling, in addition to the damage and costs.

# A SHOOTING IN GLOVERSVILLE

During the second half of the nineteenth century and early decades of the twentieth, hundreds of glovers from Somerset emigrated to the United States of America seeking a new and hopefully better life on the other side of the Atlantic Ocean; tragically one Yeovil glover on his way to that hoped-for better life, drowned in the loss of the *Titanic*. Many glovers settled in and around Gloversville, which as its name implies was a leather and glove manufacturing town in New York State, and it is here that the following events took place in the summer of 1871, causing much concern back in Somerset.

John Lucas, a sixteen-year-old Yeovil glove cutter, had left the town in 1866 eager to make his fortune in the land of promise, and had settled in Gloversville where he pursued his trade. There was a circus in town on Saturday, 17 June 1871 and as the audience turned out late in the evening, John Lucas fell in with the company of Josephine Duel and Ida Cranker, young ladies of suspect virtue, and set out for John's lodgings.

George C. Berry had been drinking hard all day, and was fairly intoxicated by the time he met up with Lucas and his two companions. Berry tried to entice the two women to go with him, but when they refused, he staggered off calling John Lucas 'a son of a bitch' and threatening to get him the next day.

At Mr Whipple's shop, where John Lucas worked and had a room, the three were joined by fellow glove cutter, William Van Rensaelear and, at about midnight, they set out to walk the two women back to their homes. Even at this late hour, the saloons and bars of Gloversville were busy and Main Street fairly crowded. William Van Rensaelear was walking with Ida Cranker a few yards ahead of John Lucas and Josephine Duel, but they had not gone far along Main Street, when they were joined by George Berry, accompanied by Marcus Dye. Both men were extremely drunk, and once again Berry tried to persuade the two women to go with them. Ida and Josephine refused, and when Berry and Dye tried to grab them, John Lucas intervened, only to be violently punched in the stomach and face by Marcus Dye. The young man from Yeovil was saved further injury by the timely intervention of another glover, William Welsh, who happened to be passing at that moment. Shouting threats to deal with Lucas at another time, Berry and Dye staggered away down Main Street.

John Lucas had been quite badly beaten, and although he was feeling faint, he joined his three friends, and they started out again for the two women's homes. They had not gone far when suddenly Berry and Dye burst from a side alley and attacked Lucas once again. Berry punched him once, but then turned his attention to Van Rensaelear and Ida Cranker. Marcus Dye grabbed John Lucas around his neck in a stranglehold, shouting that he was going to rip out his guts!

Events now happened quickly, fearing for his life, John Lucas managed to pull a small revolver from his pocket, but as he cocked it, Dye tried to wrestle the gun away and it went off. Marcus Dye let go and turning, walked down the street followed shortly after by Berry.

Thankful to have frightened Dye away, or so they thought, Lucas and Van Rensaelear saw their two female companions to their homes, but as Lucas feared another attack on his way back to his lodgings, he spent the night at his fellow glove cutter's house. Marcus Dye, however, had not let go because the shot had scared him off, but because he had a bullet lodged in his chest. He was mortally wounded, and although he managed to walk for some distance down Main Street, he finally staggered into a side alley, fell against a fence and slid to the ground. Berry ran to help his friend, and sitting him up against the fence, saw the wound and the blood and ran for a doctor. However, Dye was beyond medical help, and by the time Berry and the doctor returned, he was dead.

John Lucas was arrested the following day, and on 18 December 1871 stood trial for the murder of Marcus Dye in the courthouse of the neighbouring Johnstown. In evidence, Lucas said that he had occasionally carried a revolver because an unknown assailant had attempted to stab him one night some twelve months before. He had not meant to shoot Marcus Dye, but had feared greatly for his life during the fatal struggle, and the gun had gone off by accident. Several witnesses testified that Berry and Dye had been fighting drunk that evening, and were known to carry knives.

The trial lasted four days, and the jury was out for fourteen hours before they returned a verdict of 'Not Guilty', to the acclaim of the packed court room. It was reported that John Lucas sank down exhausted and wept like a child. Following 'excellent advice' from Judge Samuel W. Jackson on his future conduct, John Lucas was discharged and passed quietly out of the court room and the brief spotlight of history.

# THE RIOT OF 1831

During the early decades of the nineteenth century there was social and political unrest across Europe. In his book *From Portreeve to Mayor – The growth of Yeovil,* the late L.C. Hayward BA, BSc, FCA, wrote: 'Fears of popular agitation following the revolutions in Europe in 1830 and the radical movement in England showed itself in the swearing in of 250 Yeovilians as special constables in December and the forming of the Mudford Troop of Yeomanry for the protection of property... Their services were needed during the October riot in Yeovil in 1831.'

The cause of the October riot arose from the defeat of William Ponsonby, the Whig Reform candidate, by Lord Ashley in a Dorset parliamentary election at Blandford. There were allegations that Lord Ashleys agents had behaved corruptly in the election, and the protests led to rioting in Blandford and Sherborne.

Early in the evening of Friday 21 October, some youths and boys assembled in the Borough in Yeovil, shouting, 'Ponsonby and Reform for ever!' and by nine o'clock, the crowd had increased until several hundred men, women and youths, many liberally refreshed with cider and beer, were milling about. Suddenly they moved off and for a moment it was thought that the demonstration was over. However, this was wishful thinking because during the rest of the night and into the early morning a mob rampaged up and down Princes Street, Kingston and Hendford attacking, and in two cases looting, houses of Lord Ashley's supporters.

The initial assault on solicitor Mr Edwin Newman's house, in what is now Princes Street, smashed all his window panes, and then the mob broke through the front door. Despite Mr Newman threatening the invaders with a loaded pistol, they rampaged through the house, smashing furniture, stealing valuables and ransacking all the rooms. The solicitor's wife was pregnant with their third child but with her two other children she was saved from injury by the prompt action of friends who also managed to save many valuable papers from Mr Newman's office.

All the front windows of Mr Mayo's Old Sarum House in Princes Street were smashed and a few minutes later the mob stormed Mr Francis Robin's house in Ram Park (now Park Road). After smashing his windows the mob broke into the house and began to destroy furniture, bookcases, ornaments and everything they could lay their hands on, including the servants' clothes.

Articles of furniture and clothing were piled on the lawn and a bonfire lit.

Other houses attacked were those of M. White, Mr Edwin Tomkins, Mr Penny and Mr Slade, and Rev. James Hooper's Hendford Manor, and Mr John Greenham's Hendford House, but in these cases the damage was confined to broken windows.

The fury and size of the mob were too much for the town's inadequate forces of law and order, who could only stand by and watch the tide of destruction which swept up and down Princes Street and Hendford until four o'clock in the morning.

At about a quarter past eleven, local magistrate, John Goodford, whose son, returning from dining at Montacute House had witnessed the tumult, bravely rode alone into Yeovil and the riot. During that fearful night, John Goodford rode about the town, accompanied in due course by several local businessmen, and his calls for the mob to go home were partly successful. Whether this was due to Mr Goodford's exhortations or fatigue, we shall never know.

During Saturday there was a feeling of general unrest in the town, and the *Western Flying Post* reported that, 'A meeting of inhabitants was held at the Mermaid Inn, when it was resolved that all legal means should be used to prevent a repetition of such disgraceful outrages.' Several Magistrates, including Mr John Goodford, were also present at the meeting in the Mermaid. By late afternoon the crowds were once again assembling in the Borough, and the fear of further rioting was heightened by reports that people were coming in from the surrounding villages. The Magistrates therefore sent word summoning the Mudford Troop of Yeomanry cavalry to re-enforce the special constables and public officers who had proved incapable of protecting property during Friday's riot. At about a quarter to seven, news came to the Mermaid that plans were being made to attack Mr Hooper's property in Hendford, and Mr Thomas Hoskins, one of the Magistrates, read the Riot Act requiring the crowd to disperse within one hour, failing which action would be taken against them. Although this had the effect of quietening the mob they refused to disperse.

The Mudford Troop of Yeomanry, commanded by Captain George Harbin, trotted into town and formed up outside the Mermaid but the presence of the part-time cavalrymen did little to intimidate the mob. Only a few days before the Troop had been mustered – for exercise in a field on Camel Hill, where they went through their evolutions with admirable precision – and afterwards the Troop enjoyed a 'sumptuous dinner' at the Sparkford Inn. Faced with an angry mob of several hundred, the Troop realised that their evolutions would be of little use in the narrow High Street, and retired. It was reported by the *Western Flying Post* that the Mudford Troop 'left the town under the idea that their presence might be the means of bringing together a crowd.

During the commotion which followed the departure of the troop, several of the mob were arrested for throwing stones at the Mermaid and taken inside the inn. Determined efforts to release them were resisted, despite the mob trying to break through the doors and pelting the front of the inn with missiles.

The Mudford Troop had remained just outside the town, where they were re-enforced by the Martock Troop which had also been called out, commanded by Captain Tatchell. Both troops now entered the town and began to ride up and down the streets, which only increased the fury of the mob. The yeomanry came under a hail of stones and assorted missiles, and one of the troopers was knocked from his horse. The position was becoming critical when at least six shots were fired, four over the heads of the crowd and two into them. One of the yeomanry, a Mr Cottle, accidentally shot himself in the thigh and one of the mob was heard to cry out in pain. There were claims that Captain Tatchell had given the order to fire but this was subsequently denied and stated that the shots had been fired without authority.

The presence of the yeomanry probably prevented more destruction and damage to property but the crowds continued to pose a threat and it was not until a troop of regular cavalry from the 3rd Dragoon Guards trotted into Yeovil on the Sunday morning that the mob finally dispersed.

The 3rd Dragoon Guards remained in town for a fortnight, and special constables patrolled the streets from six to twelve o'clock every night for several months.

Grateful townspeople presented each member of the yeomanry with an ornate jug in recognition of their manly and forbearing character. Three of the Riot jugs are in the possession of the Museum of South Somerset – they were presented to James Masters, G. Edwards and R. Raymond.

Twenty local men and women appeared at the Somerset spring Assizes in Taunton in April 1832, charged with riotous assembly, and received sentences from six days to eighteen months; several were acquitted.

# THE SHOCKING DEATH OF SERGEANT DENTY

High on the west wall of the church of St Mary, East Chinnock, near Yeovil, a memorial tablet bears the following inscription:

Sacred to the Memory of
Captain T.S. Denty who was drowned at Peterhead,
March 6th 1881 aged 26 years
Son of the late T.D. Denty, who was killed at Yeovil
whilst drilling the Rifle Volunteers
Death comes at unexpected times,
and unexpected hours, tomorrow we may never see
today alone is ours.

What an intriguing statement: 'who was killed at Yeovil whilst drilling the Rifle Volunteers'.. No doubt many serving and former members of Her Majesty's Armed Forces, having suffered drill instruction, might conclude that the Rifle Volunteers had finally had enough drilling and assassinated their drill instructor! The facts, however, do not bear out this fantasy, although the cause of T.D. Denty's demise is not without irony.

Thomas Draper was, in fact, a sergeant of the Royal Marines, a widower with three children, and a veteran of eighteen years' service; he was also the local recruiting sergeant for the Royal Marines.

The Yeovil Rifle Volunteers were founded in 1859 and were part-time soldiers. Although these weekend warriors were keen, the volunteers were also very much a men's social club, and two of the highlights of the year were the shooting events held on the rifle range at Yeovil Marsh during October. The 1862 contest took place on Thursday 9 October, and again on the following Tuesday, the 14th, when the corps were accompanied by Sergeant Denty who had volunteered to help the target markers in the butts. As an experienced Royal Marine, Thomas Denty's presence would be welcomed by the volunteers.

Following a full morning's firing, members of the volunteers were enjoying refreshments, having just finished competing for the Ladies' Cup. The day's programme would continue after the meal, by firing on the short 300-yard range, and work was beginning on patching and rearranging targets. The volunteers did not possess two targets capable of being used separately on the long and short ranges, and it was necessary, therefore, to dismantle and take one of the large four-hundredweight (50.8kg) targets from the long range and fix it at the 300-yard butt.

Sergeant Denty and Volunteer William Grimes were busy patching and repainting the large targets, but, apart from the arrival of Volunteer Hurlston, there was no sign of the working party detailed to move the heavy target to the short range. The afternoon programme would soon be starting, but as time was running short, the sergeant decided to begin the dismantling of the target on his own, no doubt muttering at the inefficiency of the 'civilian soldiers" In trying to release one of the securing bolts, Sergeant Denty's foot slipped on the wet grass of the butt, and four-hundredweight of target came crashing down on the unfortunate Marine, breaking one of his legs.

In great pain, the sergeant was conveyed in a spring waggon on the bumpy road back to Yeovil and to his lodgings in the Butcher's Arms, where he was seen by Mr Fancourt Tomkyns, the honorary surgeon of the Rifle Volunteers, and his colleague, Dr Aldridge. By now the patient was complaining of severe abdominal pain, and despite the close attention of the two medical men, he died at half past five the same afternoon. The autopsy revealed that in addition to a badly fractured leg, the sergeant had suffered a severely damaged right kidney which had haemorrhaged into the abdomen and which was the cause of death. Ironically, Thomas Denty had enlisted in the Royal Marines on the day after Sherborne Fair, and died on the same day eighteen years later.

The inquest was held on the following day in the Three Choughs Hotel, where the Deputy Coroner, Mr Craddock, having heard the evidence of the witnesses, stated that in his opinion the death of Sergeant Denty was through no one's fault; he ought not to have tried to remove the target on his own, and was 'no doubt too adventuresome'. The jury returned a verdict of 'accidental death'. Following the inquest, the £3 fees of the jury, and the fees of the medical attendants, were handed to the sergeant's orphaned children.

On Thursday afternoon, 16 October 1862, Sergeant Thomas Draper Denty was laid to rest in Yeovil Cemetery with full military honours. During the twelve months the sergeant had been stationed in Yeovil, he had become a very popular figure, and the *Western Flying Post* reported that some 3000 people attended at the cemetery. Three volleys were fired over the grave by 18 volunteers under the command of Colour Sergeant Chaffin and Corporal Denmead, and were said to have been carried out with such precision, that persons at a distance could hardly believe that 18 rifles were discharged so simultaneously. Unfortunately, the popularity of the sergeant did not extend to providing a headstone, and he lies in an unmarked grave.

And what of his son, Captain T.S. Denty? Captain Thomas Denty was the skipper of the Bridport brig *Why Not* which was sailing in ballast to Peterhead in Scotland when she was driven onto the Skerry Rocks, and lost with all hands in a severe gale on 6 March 1881. The crew of seven were all local men: Captain Denty came from East Chinnock, the mate from Burton Bradstock on the Dorset coast, and the rest of the crew were from nearby Bridport. It was reported that the brig was an 'old one and had been for many years in the Bridport trade'.

# TEN AIR RAIDS

During the Second World War, Somerset was not spared the attentions of the German Luftwaffe. Air attacks began in July 1940, and continued with varying degrees of severity until May 1944. The cities of Bristol and Bath were heavily bombed, and suffered grievously. Attacks by bomb and gunfire on Somerset ranged from Weston-super-Mare to Castle Cary, Bridgwater to Montacute, and cost the lives of 668 of its people, with a further 1608 injured and some 35,000 buildings destroyed or damaged.

The Westland Aircraft Works at Yeovil, was an obvious target, and the town suffered ten air raids as the Luftwaffe marked the factory down for destruction.

On 30 September 1940, a force of German bombers set out to attack the Westland Aircraft Works, but heavy clouds covered the town and bombing blind, the aircraft released their deadly loads 5 miles away over Sherborne killing 18 and injuring over 30 townspeople.

However, it was only a matter of time before the Luftwaffe came back, and this they did a week later at about five minutes to four in the afternoon of Monday, 7 October. During the next few minutes high-explosive and oil-fire bombs rained destruction across the town centre and nearby residential areas. A direct hit demolished the air-raid shelter in the Vicarage Street Methodist church killing four housewives and injuring several of the 30 or so people who had taken refuge in the building. A man, two women and an eighteen-month-old toddler were trapped for a while in a cavity formed by fallen blocks of masonry, but were released relatively unharmed.

In Middle Street a bomb exploded between Montague Burton's shop and Woolworth's killing eight people, including two young men who had been playing billiards in the Saloon above Burton's. Miraculously, most of the 200 people sheltering in Woolworth's, escaped injury.

The fall of bombs across the town centre damaged shops and business premises but thankfully with no further fatalities. The *Western Gazette* reported that a young chemists assistant experienced his second bombing within a week having transferred to Yeovil from a shop in another town damaged in a raid. Ricketts' glove factory in Addlewell Lane was badly damaged but, once again, mercifully without serious casualties.

Bombs, including an oil bomb, fell on the Higher Kingston estate and a house in Roping Road was demolished. However, the bombs which fell on the western parts of Yeovil caused further deaths and injuries. Bakers' rounds-man Cyril Rendell, from West Coker, was killed in Summerleaze Park where he was delivering bread, a direct hit on an air-raid shelter in Grove Avenue killed the two occupants, and a housewife died when her house in St Andrew's Road was blown apart. An oil bomb bounced down Grove Avenue, and there was a large crater left in a vacant piece of land opposite the entrance to West Park; craters also pitted the playing fields around Summerleaze Park School. Several houses in St Andrew's Road still bear shrapnel marks from the bombs which fell nearby. There was an unexploded bomb at the junction of Preston and St Andrew's Roads, another in Park Street, and a third in the field near the balloon barrage site at Larkhill; an oil bomb which fell in Everton Road did not explode.

The *Western Gazette* reported that two insurance agents had a narrow escape when an oil bomb fell 3 feet away from the front door of one of a row of houses. It blew in the door behind which they were sheltering at the invitation of an evacuee from London, who was the only other person in the house. They were all three thrown to the floor, the door falling on top of them. Splinters from a bomb went straight through the rear of the car the men had left outside, and another large piece pierced the roof and landed on the driver's seat. Oily mud thickly bespattered the car. Luckily the bomb did not ignite although the force of the explosion was sufficient to break the concrete doorstep and tear laths from the wooden shed at the rear of the house.

The bombers were gone in minutes and when the 'all clear' sounded an hour later, 16 people were dead and 29 injured, of whom nine were serious; not one bomb had hit the Westland Aircraft Works.

The Luftwaffe came again the next evening, and between ten past seven, when the sirens wailed the alert, until the 'all clear', forty-five minutes later, some 44 high explosive bombs were scattered over the western part of Yeovil. This time Preston Grove and Westbourne Grove bore the brunt of the attack and once again the Westland factory remained unscathed. The raid left 11 dead, all killed when an air-raid shelter at the corner of Westbourne Grove and Preston Grove was totally destroyed by a direct hit. Eight of those who died, including two children, were soon identified, but early the following morning an unidentifiable adult body was found in the St Andrew's Road cul-de-sac, followed shortly after by that of a badly mutilated child in a garden in Preston Grove; five days later a mutilated female corpse was found on allot-ments by the Westland airfield. Despite extensive enquiries, the three bodies were never identified, and they were buried in Yeovil cemetery where a head-stone marks their last resting place.

The third attack on Yeovil came on Saturday evening 12 October, when a lone bomber dropped five high-explosive bombs on the town centre. Part of Church House, occupied by the solicitors, Messrs Batten & Co., was demolished and the south windows in St John's church were damaged. The *Western Gazette* reported that the glass canopy over the entrance to a picture theatre was shattered and some tiles dislodged, but that was the extent of the damage. No one in the cinema was hurt and the show went on. This was the Central Cinema in Church Street but war-time censorship forbade the naming of towns, streets and so on, in newspaper reports of air raids. The film showing at the time was *Jack's the Boy* starring Jack Hulbert and Cicely Courtneidge. The other bombs fell in Park Street and at the back of a house in Pen Hill, demolishing part of the building and damaging the adjoining South Street Infants' School; there were five reported injuries in the town.

The nearby military camp at Houndstone was bombed on 12 October when five soldiers were killed and 32 other personnel were injured, and again on the 14th, when 13 died, including Lt Col G.F.R. Wingate OBE, a relative of Major General Orde Wingate, leader of the famous 'Chindits' of the Burma campaign.

The fourth raid on the town came on 16 October when bombs fell in Mudford Road destroying five houses and injuring three occupants of No. 122. Although this would be the last attack on Yeovil in 1940, the air-raid warnings would be given on another 28 occasions before the end of the year, as the Luftwaffe passed overhead to bomb Bristol and South Wales.

In the four raids on Yeovil in 1940, 27 premises were totally destroyed and over 800 damaged, but the target, the Westland Aircraft Works remained unscathed.

At eleven o'clock on the morning of Wednesday, 26 March 1941, the air-raid warning wailed across Yeovil and one hour later at noon, a lone Dornier bomber dived across Yeovil to carry out the fifth attack on the Westland Aircraft Works, and dropped a stick of six high-explosive bombs. Four of the bombs fell in the Westland housing estate and two fell in the factory. When the 'all clear' sounded at one o'clock, three men, five women and a five-year-old boy were dead and 36 civilians injured; four of the dead were Westland employees. Eleven houses were destroyed and 132 damaged.

The official summary of the raid reported that of the two bombs which had fallen on the Westland factory, one 250kg bomb had penetrated the roof of the sub-assembly shop at an angle, struck the ground 180 feet from where it entered, ricocheted and travelled for 240 feet, exploding opposite the office building where nearly all the windows (front and back) were broken by blast. Walls were heavily marked by splinters. In the erection shop, a large number of holes made by splinters, resulted in work being held up for a night.

The second and smaller bomb of 50kg 'fell in the flying ground, skidded and exploded. Crater 4 feet x 6 feet. Water main damaged'.

Press reports of the time were heavily censored and the places raided were never named or details given of factory or business premises. The *Western Gazette*'s report of the raid is therefore brief and does not say where it occurred:

> Homes were damaged when a raider bombed and machine gunned a West Country town on Wednesday. Housewives were busily preparing the midday meal when an enemy plane dived out of the clouds and dropped its bombs on their homes. Many had miraculous escapes, but there were few casualties, some of them fatal. A twenty-year-old girl who was to have been married at Easter, was among the killed. Another victim was a child. A woman whose home was extensively damaged, escaped injury by flinging herself under a table. One young mother dashed upstairs to save her baby, and threw herself across the cradle as the bombs were falling. Although her house was damaged, mother and child were unhurt. A machine-gun attack accompanied the bombing. Bullets pierced the roof and also a window of a Roman Catholic church, and they also shattered the windows of a club room, but no one was injured. A man in a workshop had just moved away from his bench when bullets swept the spot where he had been working. Eyewitnesses say that after carrying out its bombing and machine-gunning attack, the raider appeared to open out and make off at great speed.

The author's maternal grandparents lived in Westland Road and their house was damaged, but thankfully both were unhurt. However, when his mother went to make certain they were both all right following the 'all clear', she recalled seeing a snowstorm of feathers from destroyed pillow cases and eiderdowns blowing about in the wind. The warning for the sixth raid was sounded at 9.40pm in the evening of Good Friday, 11 April 1941, and by the time of the 'all-clear', six hours later at 3.40am, several delayed-action bombs had fallen and exploded in the town centre. The Corn Exchange off High Street, and Boots the Chemist, in the Borough, were destroyed, and a large number of nearby premises, including shops, damaged. The *Western Gazette* of 18 April records:

> 'Business as usual' notices in fashion stores typified the never-say-die

spirit of local traders after high explosive bombs had been dropped by an enemy raider in a shopping district of a West Country town on the night of Good Friday. One fire blazed like a beacon light but before it could be a guide to other raiders it had been extinguished by fire-fighters, regular and auxiliary. When a high explosive made a direct hit on a three-storey shop [this was Boots the Chemist and adjoining buildings], a mother and daughter, Mrs Hawkins and Phyllis Hawkins, living in a flat on the top floor, were buried in wreckage, but after being extracted they were suffering only from shock. A bomb on another building caused a small number of casualties, some fatal. An AFS man was also injured, but chatted cheerfully to ambulance men who took him to hospital.

A fire watcher at a large shop in the rear of which an H.E. bomb fell, perhaps owes his life to the failure of the store's electricity supply. He is Bertram Francis, who was on duty with the night-watchman when a bomb of the incendiary type fell by the cloakroom in the back of the shop and caused a fire. The two men immediately set to work with a stirrup pump, but their efforts were of no avail, and the Fire Brigade was called. Meanwhile Francis went to the upstairs front of the building to try to rectify a fuse. While he was there, a bomb caused extensive damage to the rear of the shop where he had been fighting the fire previously. Part of the staircase collapsed and Francis had to make his escape by way of the roof of adjoining buildings, ending with a climb part way down the face of a shop. He was helped the rest of the way by a party of helpers. With his companion he escaped injury. A street fire watcher who is a licensee, was caught by blast, and found himself on the ground unable to move in a road strewn with broken glass and other debris. 'I wondered what on earth had happened,' he said. 'I had to crawl to a hotel, windows of which had been blown out, but I found myself quite unhurt.'

A curious experience befell a boy lying in bed in a flat over a nearby shop. The wardrobe suddenly fell across his bed with the door open. Part of the ceiling and walls collapsed, but the boy – inside the wardrobe as it were – was not touched. Another tradesman had the double misfortune of seeing the wrecking of both his shop and his house at the rear. He and his wife had to be dug out but were unhurt. Windows of two churches in the area were found pitted with jagged holes.

The *Gazette's* report 'A bomb on another building caused a small number of casualties, some fatal' referred to the one which destroyed the

Corn Exchange in which soldiers of the King's Own Scottish Borderers were billeted. Four soldiers were killed and five injured, and Patrol Officer Charles Gillard of the Auxiliary Fire Service died when the delayed-action bomb exploded as he fought the fire in the Corn Exchange. The official summary of the raid suggested that incendiary bombs had been attached to the fins of the H E bombs as the flames of the fire in the Corn Exchange were described as being of a yellow colour, as from a broken gas pipe. Water caused the fire to roar. This points to 0.9kg I.B.s attached to the fins as there were no gas mains in the vicinity.'

The Good Friday raid left five dead and 14 injured, seven buildings were totally destroyed and 182 damaged.

The Luftwaffe would return for a seventh attack at midnight on 8 May when a lone bomber swept low over the town and became caught in cable of a Royal Air Force barrage balloon at Yew Tree Close. The raider dropped its bombs but only succeeded in damaging the huts of the crew manning the balloon; there were no casualties.

On 16 May 1941, the 161st air-raid warning of the war wailed over Yeovil, and about an hour later a German bomber scattered seven high-explosive bombs from Stone Lane to Mudford Road near the junction with St Michael's Avenue. The resulting explosions caused damage to the windows and doors of some sixty houses and the Fleur de Lys hotel; thankfully there were no human casualties but one cow was killed and another injured. Yeovil had experienced its eighth air raid but a week later the ninth would be far more serious.

The air-raid warning sounded at five minutes to midnight on Saturday 24 May and when the 'all clear' sounded half an hour later, five people, including a nine-years-old boy had been killed, and seven injured. Eight houses in Mudford Road had been totally destroyed or were so badly damaged they had to be demolished, and another 115 damaged. The brief official reports of the raid state that at about two minutes past midnight a single enemy bomber dropped 14 high-explosive bombs from a very low altitude after flying three times over the town with its navigation lights on.

Because of wartime censorship, the following report in the *Western Gazette* on 30 May was also brief and could not identify the town:

When high-explosive bombs were dropped in the residential part of a West Country town on Saturday, a number of families were trapped in the wreckage of their homes. Heedless of their own safety neighbours assisted rescue squads, who worked desperately to extricate them. Casualties proved to be small, but included some killed. Among the victims were a husband and wife, and the latter's sister. A nine-year-old boy was also fatally injured.

A soldier and his wife, had a remarkable escape. The wife had already been bombed out of a bungalow at which she had been staying in another town in order to be near her husband. She returned to her own home still suffering from shock. Her husband had been given compassionate leave to be with his wife who is ill. They were both in bed when the bombs fell. The bed slid to the ground, but they were both safe, though they now have no home and nothing but what they were wearing at the time.

A man owed his life to a wardrobe which fell on him and acted as a shield when his home was hit, and in another house nearby a woman was saved from injury by a door which was blown off its hinges on top of her as the ceiling collapsed. An invalid woman was found in bed unhurt amid the ruins of her home.

The raider was met by anti-aircraft fire. After dropping its bombs it quickly made off. Salvage men, demolition crews, and other Civil Defence workers were all busy on Sunday, while husbands and wives, assisted by their children, spent the day in a great 'clean-up'.

Roy Bicknell, was four years old at the time but still remembers that night:

With my mother and father I was living at 137 Mudford Road and we were amongst those injured in the bombing of 24 May and, although I was only four years old at the time, I have a vivid memory of that night. My father was home on leave as he was serving in the Royal Navy and had just come back from India. Although it is said that the alarm was sounded at 11.55pm I believe that the bombs had fallen before the alarm was sounded. A story I was told is that in the house opposite ours lived a woman who was bedridden and they had heard the plane going round above and she said to her husband to go to the shelter, but he said no, he would stay with her and if anything was to happen it would happen to them both. Their house was hit and they ended up in the road still on the bed with only minor cuts etc., and the people in the next houses either side were killed.

I had a bad cut to my right arm which was round my father's neck as he was carrying me to my grandmother's shelter at 126 Mudford Road. We had got as far as the front gate of our home when the house opposite was hit. He also had injuries to his head and my mother had something skim over her and injure her back as we lay on the ground.

We all made a complete recovery. Our home was damaged so much that after our stay in hospital we went to live in Goldcroft until our home was fit to live in after some months.

The Luftwaffe had not quite finished with Yeovil. Wednesday, 5 August 1942, had been a pleasant summer day, but at ten minutes past nine that evening, the air raid warning sounded. Within a few minutes, two single engine Focke Wulfe fighter-bombers, roared out of the east with guns blazing and swooped low over the town. Each aircraft released one 500kg delayed-action bomb before disappearing at high speed into the west. One bomb exploded in the back gardens of houses at the junction of Gordon Road and Grass Royal, leaving a crater 5 feet deep and 26 feet wide. The second struck the ground at the rear of the Central Junior School in Reckleford, bounced into the air and over the tall leather dressing factory at the bottom of Eastland Road, to explode in Dampier Street over 200 yards away. The tenth and final raid cost Yeovil three killed and 25 injured, eight seriously; 15 houses were destroyed or had to be demolished, and 972 were damaged but repairable.

In the ten air raids on Yeovil, 49 townspeople lost their lives, and 171 were injured; 68 properties were destroyed and 2377 damaged. Warnings were sounded on 365 occasions from 5 July 1940 to 16 June 1944. Only two bombs hit the Westland Aircraft Works.

# ALL WHO GO DOWN TO
# THE SEA IN SHIPS

St Michael's church in the ancient Saxon town of Somerton is a long way from the roar of the sea, but three memorials tell the surprising stories of sailors; two of long and valiant service and one of tragedy.

Outside on the east wall of the vestry extension there is a worn memorial to thirteen-year-old Midshipman John Jacob who was drowned in the wreck of HMS *Hero* off the Dutch coast on Christmas Day 1811. In that year the Napoleonic War was at its height, and the Royal Navy was engaged in escorting convoys of merchant ships from friendly ports in the Baltic Sea to Great Britain.

A convoy of 120 ships under the protection of the 74-gun *Hero*, commanded by Captain James Newman Newman RN, and three smaller warships, set out on 18 December in fine weather for the dangerous voyage home from its Swedish anchorage in Vinga Sound. Shortly after the convoy left, the weather turned, and a few days later it was scattered by severe gales of the coast of northwest Denmark. The *Hero* and one of the escorts HMS *Grasshopper*, were left escorting 18 ships, mainly government transports, in a rapidly deteriorating situation.

At about ten o'clock on the night of 23 December in heavy squalls of snow and sleet, the ships were scattered once again. The *Hero* was close to the Dutch coast and was streaming sea anchors in an endeavour to prevent her being driven into the huge breakers crashing onto dangerous sandbanks. The northwesterly gale and high seas , however, were too powerful for the *Hero's* puny anchors and she struck the Hake Sand off the island of Texel. The ship was totally dismasted and soon mountainous waves were sweeping across her midships forcing the crew to seek sanctuary on the stern and focsle. The *Hero* fired one of her guns to attract assistance, and several small ships set out from Texel into the tremendous seas in an attempt to save the crew. Tragically none of the would-be rescuers could get within 2 or 3 miles of the stricken warship due to the raging seas and strong tides flowing onto the shore.

The *Grasshopper* had also been driven towards the lethal sandbanks, but had been able to gain safety within a more sheltered stretch of water. Her crew made valiant attempts to rescue their shipmates on the *Hero*, but the surf was too high and all efforts were in vain. During that long Christmas Day, the men of the *Grasshopper* were forced to remain as helpless spectators whilst the

*Hero* and her gallant crew, including thirteen-year-old Midshipman John Jacob, were washed away and drowned in the raging surf off the Dutch coast.

One of John Jacob's shipmates on that terrible day, was twenty-one-year-old Thomas Russell Munden, the third son of the rector of Corscombe, a village some 20 miles from Somerton in the Dorset Hills, where a memorial in the parish church of St Mary remembers the loss of this young man in the wreck of the *Hero*.

Tragically, Midshipman Jacob was not to see long service in the Royal Navy, unlike the brothers George and William Tremlett, whose memorials are displayed side by side in the chancel of St Michael's. Commander George Neate Tremlett died on 20 April 1865 at the great age of ninety-seven years, and his memorial relates that at the time of his death he was the oldest officer in the Royal Navy which he joined in 1780. George Tremlett began his long naval career at Exmouth when he joined the 14-gun warship HMS *Beaver* as a master's servant to her captain, Joseph Peyton, and his first taste of action was against the French in 1781 on board HMS *Medway*. As a Lieutenant on HMS *Penguin* in August 1797, he won the praise of his captain for his brave conduct during the running fight with the *Oiseau*, a French privateer, which was eventually captured.

His brother William Henry Brown Tremlett, who eventually reached the rank of vice-admiral, had an equally long naval career, and died some six months after George on 11 November 1865, at the advanced age of ninety-four years. William's service in the Royal Navy was full of incident and on many occasions he came close to losing his life. One such brush with death occurred off Malaga where, as a young officer, he was engaged in a fight with an armed Greek vessel. William Tremlett was in command of three small boats attacking the larger ship, and came under heavy fire. Two of the boats broke off the fight and retreated, leaving William in the one remaining to become the focus of the Greeks' fire. With most of his crew of 20 killed or wounded, he finally withdrew and reached safety. During the fight William's hat was holed in seven places and the handle of his dirk shot off.

By 1808, William Tremlett had reached the rank of captain, but whilst on exercise with the Sea Fencibles (a naval home defence force) he was accidentally wounded in the right foot by a blast of grape shot, and one piece of shot weighing half a pound remained lodged there for two and a half years before it was removed; his application for a pension for the wound was refused!

In June 1808, Captain Tremlett took command of HMS *Alcmene*, and joined the fleet blockading the French coast. Three days before Christmas 1808, two large French frigates came into view, and the *Alcmene* set out to capture them. Both Frenchmen turned and ran for shelter. The chase lasted over 130 miles, when finally the two frigates found shelter under the guns of the French garrison of St Martin's Citadel on the Ile de Re off La Rochelle. Captain Tremlett was not to be cheated of his prey, and the following night he planned to run alongside the frigate nearest to the open sea, board and capture her. The *Alcmene* silently approached the enemy ship and the operation seemed to be going to plan when suddenly, within yards of the Frenchman, Tremlett's ship shuddered to a halt. She was aground less than a pistol shot from her target, which it transpired was also aground! The situation was now very dangerous because the noise caused by the efforts to refloat the *Alcmene* had roused the citadel's garrison who opened fire on the British man-o'-war. Fortunately the ship was quickly refloated and escaped without suffering too much damage.

During the rest of the winter of 1808–9, Captain Tremlett and the *Alcmene*, continued to operate off the Atlantic coast of France as part of the blockading fleet. On 29 April, a French frigate was sighted and the *Alcmene* set off in pursuit. The chase lasted throughout the day when suddenly at the mouth of the River Loire there was a crash and the *Alcmene* came to a shuddering stop, she had run onto a sunken reef. With her bottom ripped out, the *Alcmene* quickly sank, and the French frigate escaped. Fortunately Captain Tremlett and his crew were rescued by another British ship, and although the failure of navigation was blamed on the *Alcmene*'s French pilot, who was working for the Royal Navy, this was the captain's last command in the war.

# REFERENCES AND SOURCES

THE DEADLY BELLOWS MAKER
J.W. Sweet, *The Somerset Magazine*, January 1995.

AN AUTUMN STORM
*Bridgwater Mercury*, 9, 16 and 23 October 1895.
*Pulman's Weekly News*, 8 and 15 October 1895.
*Western Gazette*, 11 October 1895.
*Bridgwater & the River Parrett in Old Photographs*, compiled by Rod Fitzhugh, Alan Sutton Publishing, Phoenix    Mill, Stroud, Gloucester, 1993.
Steamship *Tender* – photographs page 52.

A FATAL FOOTBALL GAME
J.W. Sweet, *Yeovil Times*, 19 January 2000.

DEATH DOWN THE PIT
*Bath Chronicle*, 29 June and 6 July 1843.
*Taunton Courier,* 28 June 1843.

POACHERS AND POLICE
J.W. Sweet, *Yeovil Times*, 8 March 2000.

THE FORGER OF MARK
*Bath Chronicle*, 16 April 1818.
*Taunton Courier*, 20 August and 10 September 1818.

A FOE FOR A FRIEND
J.W. Sweet, *South Somerset News and Views*, January 1990.

LOVELY WOMEN, FAIR BUT FALSE
J.W. Sweet, *Yeovil Times*, 20 March 2002.

THREE SHOCKING MURDERS
J.W. Sweet, *South Somerset News and Views*, January 1999.
*Western Flying Post*, 27 November and 4 December 1809, 9 April 1810, 6 and 13 April 1816.

*Bath and Cheltenham Gazette*, 10 April 1816.
*Taunton Courier*, 11 April 1816.

FRAUDSTERS
J.W. Sweet, *Yeovil Times*, 12 May 1999.

A DEATH FROM NEGLECT
*Yeovil Times*, 21 November 2001.

GORE LANGTON'S OLD TROUSERS AND OTHER SURPRISING
STORIES
J.W. Sweet, *South Somerset News and Views*, March 1991, March 1998 and
October 1998.
J.W. Sweet, *Yeovil Times,* 20 February 2002.

FIRE!!
J.W. Sweet, *Yeovil Times*, 10 February 1999 and 17 October 2001.

THE WIDCOMBE BRIDGE DISASTER
J.W. Sweet, *Yeovil Times*, 21 June 2000.
*Western Gazette*, 6, 15, 22 and 29 June and 20 July 1877.
*Pulman's Weekly News*, 12 June 1877.

THE STONING OF A SCHOOLMASTER
J.W. Sweet, *Yeovil Times*, 23 June 1999.

DANGEROUS ENGINES OF DESTRUCTION
J.W. Sweet, *South Somerset News and Views*, November 1990 and June 1999.

A SUPPOSED CASE OF POISONING
J.W. Sweet, *South Somerset News and Views*, August 1999.

GILES HUTCHINGS ESCAPES
*Western Gazette*, 4 May 1878, 18 and 25 November, and 16 December 1881.

THE NOTORIOUS MAGGS AND SPARROW
*Bath Chronicle*, 8 April 1851.
*Taunton Courier*, 30 June and 3 November 1852, 23 March, 6 April and 18
August 1853.
*Western Flying Post*, 24 September, 21 and 28 October, 4 and 11 November

1851, 13 April 1852, 25 March and 5 April 1853.

THE TRIAL OF MRS JANE LEIGH PERROT
*Bath Chronicle*, 3 April 1800.
*Bath Journal*, 7 April 1800.
*Western Flying Post*, 7 April 1800.
*The Trial of Jane Leigh Perrot – Reported by John Pinchard, Attorney of Taunton*,
printed by Thomas Norris at Taunton, 1800.
*Somerset and Dorset Notes and Queries*, 1924, pp 1–8, 58–61, 99–105, and
135–138.

ARSON AT DUNSTER
*Western Flying Post*, 17 August 1818. 1990.

HE DYED IN THE KING'S SERVICE
J.W. Sweet, Private papers.

THE CASE OF THE STOLEN TOOTH EXTRACTORS
J.W. Sweet, *Yeovil Times*, 25 January 2002.

THE SURPRISING ADVENTURES OF A MONMOUTH REBEL
J.W.Sweet, *Somerset Magazine*, November 1994.

JAMES MARTIN AND THE FLOOD OF '94
J.W. Sweet, *South Somerset News and Views*, January 2001.
*Pulman's Weekly News*, 20 November 1894.

DEATHS ON THE LINE
J.W. Sweet, *South Somerset News and Views*, July 2001.

THE FIGHT AT PYE CORNER
J.W. Sweet, *South Somerset News and Views*, March 2000.

A HORRID MURDER IN BATH
*Western Flying Post*, 4, 11 and 18 February, 14 April, 12 May, 2 and 9 June
1828.
*Bath Chronicle*, 7 February 1828.
*Bath and Cheltenham Gazette*, 28 January, 5 February, 15 April, 6, 13, 20 and 27
May and 10 June 1828.

IF ONLY THEY HAD BEEN ABLE TO SWIM
J.W. Sweet, *South Somerset News and Views*, September 1995.
THE FATAL FIGHT AT THE QUEEN'S HEAD
The *Western Flying Post*, 18 and 24 November 1843.

TWO HUNTS AND A SURPRISING ESCAPE
J.W. Sweet, *Somerset Magazine*, August 1992.

UP BEFORE THE BENCH
*Western Flying Post*, 26 February 1857 and 17 July 1871.

A SHOOTING IN GLOVERSVILLE
J.W. Sweet, *Yeovil Times*, 25 November 1998.

THE RIOT OF 1831.
J.W. Sweet, *Yeovil Times*, 20 October 1999.

THE SHOCKING DEATH OF SERGEANT DENTY
J.W. Sweet, *Somerset Magazine*, March 1995.

TEN AIR RAIDS
J.W. Sweet, *Yeovil Times*, 4 October 2000, 28 March and 16 May 2001.
J.W. Sweet, Private papers.
Mac Hawkins, *Somerset at War 1939–1945*, The Dovecote Press, Stanbridge,
Wimborne, Dorset, 1988.

ALL WHO GO DOWN TO THE SEA IN SHIPS
J.W. Sweet, *Somerset Magazine*, April 1996.
*Pulman's Weekly News*, 20 November 1894.